CHEROKEE ASTROLOGY

Animal Medicine in the Stars

RAVEN HAIL

Bear & Company
Rochester, Vermont

Bear & Company
One Park Street
Rochester, Vermont 05767
www.BearandCompanyBooks.com

Bear & Company is a division of Inner Traditions International

Originally published in 2000 by Destiny Books under the title *The Cherokee Sacred Calendar: A Handbook of the Ancient Native American Tradition*

Library of Congress Cataloging-in-Publication Data
Hail, Raven.
[Cherokee sacred calendar]
Cherokee astrology : animal medicine in the stars / Raven Hail.
p. cm.
Originally published: Cherokee sacred calendar. Rochester, Vt. : Destiny Books, c2000.
Summary: "Explains the ancient astrological system sacred to the Cherokee and how to use it in the modern world"—Provided by publisher.
ISBN-13: 978-1-59143-087-2 (pbk.)
ISBN-10: 1-59143-087-9 (pbk.)
1. Cherokee calendar. 2. Cherokee astronomy. 3. Cherokee Indians—Religion. I. Title.

E99.C5H218 2008
970.004'97—dc22

2007045042

Printed and bound in the United States

10 9 8 7 6 5

Text design and layout by Jon Desautels and Virginia Scott Bowman
This book was typeset in Garamond Premiere Pro and Gil Sans with Papyrus as the display typeface

With The Awakening of The People
        to the Voice of the Immortals,
and the Gathering of Eagles
        at the Place of our Beginnings
comes the message of The Mountains
        which shall be to all people:
Cherokee spirituality
        is not just for Cherokees—
It is for
THE CHILDREN OF MOTHER EARTH!

CONTENTS

The Cherokee
Sacred Calendar

What's in a name? That which we call a rose
*By any other name would smell as sweet . . .**

That is the question posed by Romeo and Juliet, those highborn, star-crossed lovers of so long ago.

"Not so," according to a great many people of a great many other times and places.

"Your name is everything: the essence of your being; your very heart and soul," would be the answer given by The People. The People includes all Cherokee people, The Seven Clans—and in its largest sense, could be stretched out to include any or all people everywhere. Cherokees called themselves *Aniyunwiya;* translated into English this means principal people, most important people, chosen people—in other words "The People." All other people who claim to be non-Cherokees (strangers, enemies?) were simply referred to as "the other people."

At the Time of the Discovery of The Cherokees (1540, by DeSoto) we were a matriarchal, matrilineal people, divided into seven clans; the mother and all her children (male and female) belonged to her clan. But not the father; he was not even blood kin; he belonged to the clan of his mother. Sons and daughters were identified by their current name, followed by: whose mother is _____. One might say "I am *Galagina* (Buck), son of *Oganunitsi* (Groundhogs' Mother)." Or "I am Galagina, whose mother is Oganunitsi." Identification of an individual as daughter/son of the father is a custom with current patriarchal cultures.

A bit of Cherokee humor is: "We know who your mother is; who your father is, is only rumor." The widespread "old wives' tale" was

---

* William Shakespeare, *Romeo and Juliet,* act II, scene 2.

that Grandfather Moon was the father of all children. This delightful notion is not to say that we did not know about the birds and the bees; it is comparable to today's popular concept that the stork brings babies. Surely only the babies believe this. Some say they were borne of a cabbage leaf—personally, I was found on a lily pad.

Back in those days, the name of every newborn child was determined by the Sacred Venus Calendar of Natal Days. The Daykeeper calculated the name and passed this information on to the mother by way of a midwife. The midwife had the responsibility to see that the mother immediately called her child by name and baptized it with her own milk. This rite must be performed immediately. That is of course B.S.* If a baby dies without a name, it will be lost forever in the ether of the cosmos.

If this sounds like a far-out fancy of The People, it is not. Many cultures of the world have similar beliefs. Some Christians of the past (and even the present) teach that an unbaptized infant goes straight to hell, and is therefore denied burial in sacred ground.

One's Cherokee name was very sacred and equally secret. When the first U.S. census takers demanded names of Cherokee individuals, they would not reveal their secret names. Most of them had to be threatened with jail terms before they relented. A compromise was finally reached, and it operated like this: a possible English name was suggested; the Cherokee accepted it, and that was what the census taker wrote down. This resulted in a great many later Cherokee names like Boudinot, Bushyhead, Rogers, and Smith. Sometimes, through misunderstanding, a man ended up with his mother's maiden name. Such names in the native language did not seem strange to the man; only the translator was confounded.

One's name could be changed, whenever necessary, with proper ceremony. One example of such an occasion is when the Medicine Woman's diagnosis is that an illness is terminal. As a last resort, the patient is given a new name and the old name dies, while the

---

*before spanking

person with the new name lives on. Other cultures have similar beliefs. An Asian student informed me that her father had such an experience. He was given a limited time to live, but on receiving a new name, he lived to a ripe old age.

When a person dies, the name also dies. It is not to be spoken. To say the name would keep the spirit earthbound, and tempt it to hover over the physical world. It is right (*duyugdun*) to let a spirit go free, to enter The Way, to pursue its own destiny.

When the name is again given to a living entity, the taboo is lifted.

An essential part of the Cherokee Religion is the belief that every single thing in this world is an Earth-reflection of a Star. This includes not only people and animals but inanimate things such as rivers, stones, trees, and flowers.

The Lord of the Dance is the North Star (Polaris at the present time). Around the Lord of the Dance, The Heavens dance in a never-ending circle. Those who have attended the so-called Cherokee stomp dances know that the Dancers dance in a circle around The Fire. Male and female Dancers alternate all around the circle, with the female Turtle Shakers at the beginning of the line. This turns out to be a corkscrew at the big dances, with the more important persons at the head of the line and the lesser in importance on down the line, with the novices and children dancing at the very tail end—on the outside of the circle and farthest away from The Fire.

In the same manner, the Stars move around the Lord of the Dance.

Not all Cherokee Dances are in a Circle—just most of them, and particularly the Social Dances. The Ant Dance and Booger Dance, for example, follow a somewhat different pattern, but the audience sits in a circle around the performers.

There are Twelve Winds, named Hummingbird, Shrike, Lark, Quail, Sandpiper, Woodpecker, Bat, Shitepoke, Snowbird,

Blackbird, Bluebird, and Purple Martin, who dance around the circle. Each Bird is represented by a Star in one of the twelve zodiacal signs along the Ecliptic. The Thirteenth Bird is the Lead Dancer— Woodcock, *Agalu'ga* 'Thou Whirlwind'. His Place of Abode is Coma Berenices, the North Galactic Pole of The Universe.

The Little Dipper is an Adze of meteoric iron in the hands of the Lord of the Dance with which he shapes the destiny of Earth.

The constellation Draco is *Ukte'na,* Dragon, who is guardian of the North Star and Keeper of the Magic Crystal stone.

The Milky Way is Long Man, The River. On Earth he is The River of Life, and in the sky he is The River of Death, or The Path of Souls. Upon death, each Entity travels along the Milky Way and must pass *Agise'gwa,* the Great Mother Dog, whose Place of Abode is Sirius the dog star. At the end of the Path of Souls, one must pass *Wa'hyaya',* the other Great Mother Wolf, whose Place of Abode is Antares. The Soul who cannot propitiate these two Spirits is caught in the backwash of the current's ebb and flow.

Agise'gwa and Wa'hyaya' fill the same roles as Anubis and Upuaut, twin Jackal Gods of the Egyptian Otherworld.

All dogs are domesticated wolves. In the very earliest myths, Sirius and Antares were the Wolf Stars. But dogs have been around for so very long that they have replaced wolves in the myths. One of the few bits of information that has been passed on to the general public in this century is that the Milky Way is "Where The Dog Ran." The Cherokee word for a physical dog has been used. Changes like this occur over the millennia—Sirius is now known as the Dog Star and Antares is the eye of the scorpion. Day Signs of this Calendar were here before dogs.

The Northern Cross is the Tree of Life beside the Milky Way River and perched atop it is the Star Deneb, who is *Guwi'sguwi,* the Cherokee Heron Spirit Bird, comparable to the Egyptian Phoenix. One myth has it that a beautiful young maiden (the Heron Spirit Bird) fell from the Tree of Life in the Sky Vault, and found no place to land on the Primordial Sea. Turtle came to the surface of the water and gave her a place to land. She nested there and laid her Cosmic Egg, from which came all life on Earth.

The three Stars of the belt of Orion make up *Dak'si,* Turtle, who carries Turtle Island (North America) on her back. El Nitak, one of these three Stars, is the Cherokee Cosmic Egg, the Place of Emergence of each New World in the never-ending cycle of time.

On down the Milky Way River is Serpens, which is the Cherokee Spirit Serpent, *Do'tsi.* And:

> Rainbow is the tongue
> of the Celestial Serpent
> flicking off the rain.*

The Big Dipper is combined with four Stars of the constellation Boötes to form the Bear (bowl of the Big Dipper) with the Seven Hunters, *Ani'kana'ti,* chasing it. These Hunters are the three Stars of the dipper handle: Robin, Chickadee (with a *Tusti* pot to cook the Bear in), and Buzzard, who means to help eat the meat after it is prepared. Then, in Boötes, there are Pigeon, Blue Jay, Owl (Arcturus), and Sparrow—who of course is the pigtail, and always gets only the crumbs.

Yona the Bear emerges from the Bear's Den, *Usta'galuni* (Corona Borealis), in early spring, and the Seven Hunters follow after. This goes on year after year after year, for the Cherokees had hunted Bear as long as they could remember. Bear meat was considered a great delicacy.

The Pleiades are the Seven Boys, *Anitsutsa,* who would rather dance than eat. They regulate planting and harvesting. The Cherokee New Year is determined by the Pleiades, and also planting time in the spring. These Stars are sometimes referred to as

---

*From *Ravensong* (book and cassette) by Raven Hail.

the Four Hundred Boys, but since there are in reality thousands of Stars in this particular cluster, one wonders why "seven" and "four hundred" are the numbers counted. Possibly seven because it stands for "all there is, everywhere":

These four:
East, North, West, South—
with Spirit High, Earth Low,
and the Center-of-Being, make
Seven!*

The Cherokee myth is that The People came to Earth originally from the Pleiades, specifically Alcyone, the brightest Star in the cluster. Strangely enough, some present-day astronomers have put forth the theory that Alcyone is the center of the universe, but that idea hasn't caught on generally. When astronomy becomes more advanced, possibly everyone will agree with the Cherokees on this point.

The Pleiad Month in the Cherokee Solar Calendar is November, or more specifically, from October 23 to November 21, the time now given for the astrological sign Scorpio. (The sign changes every two thousand years or so.)

The Ball Game, which was played under the Full Moon, originated as an imitation of celestial motion, with the Ball representing the Moon.

Cherokee *Noqui'si Sheena,* the Demon Star that winks, is Algol. He is a frustrated lover who keeps sneaking back to Earth to look for his girlfriend.

Venus, The Great Horned Rabbit, is The Twins, one manifestation of the Dual Polarities of life: Morning Star and Evening Star. Other manifestations are The Hero Twins, Reed and Flint; *Chaga'see* and *Chawa'see* (Pollux and Castor), the Medicine Men

---

*From *Ravensong.*

who carried the Redbird Daughter of The Sun back from The Darkening Land in *Gunesun'ee,* The Wooden Box (Gemini); and The Drum and The Drumstick, brother and sister "Little People."

Comets, Meteorites, and Novas are called "Fire Panther" because they breathe fire like the Panther, and are Omens of Disaster. A meteoric shower in 1833 was the forerunner of the Cherokee "Trail of Tears" from Tennessee to Indian Territory (Oklahoma).

Over and above all is The Goddess, *Ghigau* "The Red Woman," The Sun, with Her alter ego, Fire; Her familiar animal, Panther; and Her bird, Dove.

And Her Prince Consort Brother, Grandfather Moon, with his alter ego, The River; his sons, the Two Little Red Men of Thunder; his familiar animal, Wolf; and his bird, Raven.

It was the belief that upon death, an Entity was carried up to the Sky Vault to shine there as a Star. For each person is an Earth-reflection, a Shadow, an Emanation, of a particular Star that holds a permanent place in The Heavens.

Death is equated with The Sun setting in the west; She enters the Otherworld of Night, and remains there until it is time to emerge into the light of another day.

The Cherokee Sacred Calendar is a Venus Calendar of 260 days: 20 individual Day Signs and 13 Numbers (20 × 13 = 260). The Venus year is not the time it takes Venus to orbit the Sun, which is 225 days (or so) if you are on the planet Venus and 584 days if you are on planet Earth. I use the number of days as calculated from Earth, because I don't know anyone who lives on Venus.

Venus appears as The Morning Star for a little over 260 days and as The Evening Star for a little over 260 days. This is also the approximate gestation time of the human fetus. It is interesting to note here that everything in Nature is "approximately," "a little over," or "just less than." Nothing comes out as a whole number. The time it takes for the Earth to orbit the Sun is 365.24220 days (but that's an "or so" also).

The Moon takes anywhere from 27 to 30 days to orbit the Earth—depending on whether the time is calculated relative to Earth, the Solar System, or the Stars.

The Cherokee Solar New Year started with the heliacal setting of the Pleiades Star Cluster, but it was celebrated on the first New Moon afterward, which was sometime around November 1. The Pleiades culminates (reaches directly overhead at midnight) around the middle of November, and that was another important date; the Leonid Meteoric Shower around that time each year sets off fireworks to celebrate the New Year.

The heliacal rising of the Pleiades around May 1 each year marked the time for the planting season to begin. And the Green Corn Dance was in late July or early August, depending on when the New Moon was first sighted.

It was the business of the olde-time Cherokee Daykeeper to coordinate the Venus Calendar, the Solar Calendar, and the Lunar Calendar, and to select a fortunate Day for each New Moon Ceremony. They fudged a little sometimes; but since most present-day holidays are being observed on the nearest Friday or Monday, that seems to be the way to go.

The Twenty Day Signs are listed below. The English name of the Sign is followed by the Cherokee name written in English and in the Cherokee alphabet.

TURTLE—Dak´si—ꮣꭺꮈ

WHIRLWIND—Agalu´ga—ꭰꭶꮅꭶ

HEARTH—O´ya—ꭳꮿ

DRAGON—Ukte´na—ꭴꭹꭤꮎ

SERPENT—Do´tsi—ꮩꮟ

TWINS—Takato´ka—ꮤꭶꮩꭶ

DEER—Ahwu´sdi—ꭰꮼꮝꮧ

RABBIT—Noqui´segwa´—ꮒꮖꮞꮖ

THE RIVER—Yun'wi Gunnahi'ta—B ☉ E☉ ☊ W

WOLF—Kana'ti—☽ ☉ Ꭻ

RACCOON—Kvh'li—E Ꮛ

RATTLESNAKE TOOTH—Kanu'ga—☽ ꟼ Ꮥ

REED—I'hya—T ☊ Ꮿ

PANTHER—Saho'ni—Ꮀ Ꮝ h

EAGLE—Uwo'hatli—☾ ☯ Ꮞ Ꮯ

OWL—U'guku'—☾Ꭻ Ꭻ

HERON—Guwi'sguwi—Ꭻ ☉ Ꮿ Ꭻ ☉

FLINT—Dawi'sgala—Ꮮ ☉ Ꮿ Ꮥ W

REDBIRD—Totsu'hwa—V Ꭻ Ꮐ

FLOWER—Gun'tsi—E Ꮶ

The days move around in a circle that really has no beginning and no end. They maintain exactly the same relationship to each other as indicated in the drawing here, and the circle was usually shown in this position. The top of the circle is the direction East, for Cherokees are always going toward success and happiness—no matter what the actual geographical direction. Time periods were commonly called by the name of the last day in the period, instead of the first day, as is the current custom. Flower here is the last glyph, which is the position of most importance. And the last named includes "all of the above"; Flower represents The Sun and all twenty of these are solar days.

Heron is in the center as well as in the circle of Days, for time-wise we are now in the World of Heron and this particular glyph marks the Center-of-Being.

When the new Sun (World, Eon, Age) appears, the Heron glyph will be replaced by the glyph of the World that is next in line. This will not necessarily be Flint, which always follows Heron in the circle of Days. The line of succession of Worlds is much more complicated than that.

The twenty Days move around the circle Earthwise (counter-clockwise) in the direction of and in sync with the rotation of the Earth. This is also the direction of the Ceremonial Dance around The Fire in the center; the Dancers face the anticipated rising Sun whose appearance at dawn marks the end of the dancing and the beginning of the "Going to the Water" ceremony.

One lunar day is thirteen solar days. A lunar month is 28 solar days. A Venus year is 260 solar days. A solar year is 360 solar days (the same as 360 degrees in any circle) plus 5 or 6 solar days until the heliacal setting of the Pleiades. A lunar year is—let me see now—let's think about that tomorrow!

Top—East

Finding Your Own Natal Day

To find your own Natal Day, it is important to remember that the Day Signs follow one another in the same order, no matter how the Thirteen Numbers occur. The Days may be seen as going around in a circle (see p. 11) so when you start anywhere in the circle they keep the same relationship with each other. You count them going around counterclockwise.

You will need the month, day, and year of your birth. The Cherokee Day begins at sunrise (at the place of your birth) so if you were born after midnight and before sunrise, your birthday falls on the previous day. If you were born in the summertime any year from 1919 on, you need to take daylight savings time into consideration when calculating the time of sunrise at your birthplace.

Remember that 1900 was *not* a leap year, but starting with 1904, every fourth year, including 2000, is a leap year and therefore February has 29 days instead of 28. Now you can use the ephemeris that begins on page 128 to determine your Natal Day. Here is an example of how it works. If you were born May 15, 1961 (after sunrise), find the two dates immediately before and immediately after that date in the ephemeris. Thus:

May 10, 1961, and May 23, 1961

Write those two dates on a sheet of lined paper, with 13 spaces in between, like this:

May 10, 1961	–	1	**DEER**
May 11, 1961	–	2	RABBIT
May 12, 1961	–	3	THE RIVER
May 13, 1961	–	4	WOLF
May 14, 1961	–	5	RACCOON
May 15, 1961	–	6	**RATTLESNAKE TOOTH**
May 16, 1961	–	7	REED

May 17, 1961	–	8	PANTHER
May 18, 1961	–	9	EAGLE
May 19, 1961	–	10	OWL
May 20, 1961	–	11	HERON
May 21, 1961	–	12	FLINT
May 22, 1961	–	13	REDBIRD
May 23, 1961	–	1	**FLOWER**

You can see here that your Natal Day is 6 Rattlesnake Tooth. (Unless you were born between midnight and sunrise on that date—in which case your Natal Day is 5 Raccoon.)

Here is another example. If your birthday is June 21, 1953 (after sunrise):

June 15, 1953	–	1	**TURTLE**
June 16, 1953	–	2	WHIRLWIND
June 17, 1953	–	3	HEARTH
June 18, 1953	–	4	WOLF
June 19, 1953	–	5	SERPENT
June 20, 1953	–	6	TWINS
June 21, 1953	–	7	**DEER**
June 22, 1953	–	8	RABBIT
June 23, 1953	–	9	THE RIVER
June 24, 1953	–	10	WOLF
June 25, 1953	–	11	RACCOON
June 26, 1953	–	12	RATTLESNAKE TOOTH
June 27, 1953	–	13	REED
June 28, 1953	–	1	**PANTHER**

Here your Natal Day is 7 Deer. If you were born between midnight and sunrise, it will be 6 Twins.

Once you have calculated half a dozen or so Natal Days, you will find it only takes about five minutes—even less if you're a whiz kid!

The Twenty
Day Signs

Provided in this part, for each of the twenty Day Signs, is the English name of the Sign, the Cherokee name written in English, and the Cherokee name using the Cherokee alphabet. This is followed by an outline of the Sign's seven correspondences: Direction, Symbol, Color, Stone, Element, Flower, and Herb. The main description combines ancient Cherokee teachings with the qualities and attributes of those born under the particular Sign. Each section ends with The Shadow Dance, which provides an overview of the specific challenges facing the Sign.

Refer back to the Contents page to find the page number on which your Day Sign description begins.

TURTLE

DAK'SI

Ꮣ Ꮝ Ꮟ

Direction: East—Creative focus at the one-on-one, personal level; solitude; dawn: awakening, birth.

Symbol: Turtle Island

Color: Burgundy—Wine of New Life

Stone: Pearl

Element: Water

Flower: Wine cup (red poppy mallow)

Herb: Groundhog's forehead (trailing arbutus)

The Turtle constellation in the Sky is the Belt of Orion; one of these three Stars is the Cosmic Egg. At the beginning of each new Era, it appears with the rising Sun and heralds the Creation of a new World.

The Old Ones say that once a Star fell from the Sky Vault, down, down, down, through the air toward the churning waters below. Turtle came up from the depths and hung suspended on the surface to provide a landing place.

The Turtle's back grew and flourished and became Turtle Island—North America; The Star was the Cosmic Egg from which emerged all life on Earth. And so Turtle is equated with Mother Earth—The Cradle of Life.

Creativity is the forte of this Natal Day Sign. It indicates a person who is suspended in time and space, but well centered and somewhat stationary. This person is able to see the dark world of the waters below, through the veil of the psyche of the unconscious, into the mystery of the mind, from which is the beginning of all life.

The Turtle may remain absolutely motionless for long periods of time, and is slow to move even when prodded. Those of this Day Sign are inclined to look before they leap, and especially to think carefully before changing the usual direction. They do not waste time dithering; each action is performed with a full measure of value received for energy expended.

Being so closely associated with the Earth and its bounty, those of this Sign are greatly concerned with material things. They enjoy good food and drink; sometimes it becomes their main interest in life. Some may be expert cooks to the extent of raising wining and dining to a fine art. They may make a profession of gourmet food preparation, as a master chef or television cooking demonstrator. They are very good at service professions—helping, nurturing, and protecting others. Turtle types are natural leaders, sometimes founders of nonprofit service organizations.

Turtle does not take orders well, and therefore is more success-ful at the head of a small company, rather than as an employee of a large corporation. Farmer, soldier, tradesman, insurance agent, are good positions for this type.

They are very successful in working out their own ideas, but dismal failures in cooperative endeavors. Yet they are very nurtur-ing, not only to their fellow man, but to all fellow creatures.

This Sign is a perfect example of inertia: at rest until moved to action—or moving along in the same old rut until some external agent forces a change. This is typically Cherokeean behavior; there is a verb suffix in our language that means: ". . . came for the pur-pose of doing this, am now doing the same, and will continue to do so until something happens to stop it."

Honest, reliable, efficient. Bold and passively obstinate. A posi-tive personality. Turtles demonstrate "true grit," with the physical and mental power to stand up for their own convictions. Strong as the Rock of Gibraltar and equally unmovable. A mound of solid ground in the swirling whirlpool of the modern world.

They are likely to acquire wealth and hold on to it; very security-conscious, careful always to have a roof overhead and an extra string to their bow; not given to taking chances—gamblers who only bet on a sure thing; physical and financial "fat cats."

Those of this Sign have a great need for privacy. They don't like to be pushed and shoved or crowded. They're more likely to be introverted than extroverted. If annoyed, they withdraw into their shells. When nagged, they are likely to clam up completely.

They have strong intuition. In addition to maternal instinct, some appear to be psychic. They are attracted to the contemplative and oracular, and to science fact or fiction. When they follow their own hunches, they are very likely to be successful. Possibly living proof that genius is 10 percent inspiration and 90 percent perspira-tion. For when they have the proper incentive, they can truly move mountains.

The tough shell is to protect their tender inner feelings from what they see as a cold, cruel world. They need their own private place to retire to when the outside pressure builds up. Otherwise they may become a cocklebur—and then others give them their space, even in the middle of a crowd.

Turtle is a manifestation of the feminine principle of the Universe, which is the peaceful, agricultural, small-village lifestyle. At the Cherokee "stomp dances" only the women wear terrapin-shell rattles on their legs and are called Turtle Shakers. Around The Fire (also feminine) in the center, they alternate in line with the men dancers and move in a circle, counter-sunwise. They stomp their feet against the Earth, producing a very satisfactory sound.

Turtle (or terrapin) shells are used by Medicine Women and Men for mixing and storing the herbal medicines used in curing ceremonies.

Turtle Signs are sometimes confused with the lotus-eaters who dream life away and never accomplish anything at all. Not so. In the fable of the Tortoise and the Hare, it was not the flashy, over-confident bragging of the Hare, but the slow-moving, diligent, single-minded, bulldog tenacity of the Turtle that won the race.

Turtle is the Sign of Universal Unity. It is the "e pluribus unum—from all, one" of the seal of the United States. It is the source, the beginning, the Creation. In the Circle of Life it follows The End, and therefore is also the embodiment of Re-Creation, or Everlasting Life.

THE SHADOW DANCE

There is a Power that rules the Universe; it affects everyone, whether they believe it or not. If you are on your knees in the abyss of endless night, faith in this Power enables you to stand straight up and walk straight forward—when all around it is so dark you can't see a thing. Loss of Faith is catastrophic.

There is a tendency for those of this Sign to be overprotective and overbearing, which leads to a power struggle.

True, it is more blessed to give than to receive (more fun, too), but Turtle types are sometimes too proud to accept help of any kind. If you give to others something that is not good enough for yourself, you have given nothing. Learn to receive graciously. And to state clearly what you want or need.

There is a difference between meditation and daydreaming. Impatience, laziness, and procrastination can sneak up on you.

WHIRLWIND

AGALU'GA

D S M S

Direction: North—An inquiring mind; learning, training, teaching.

Symbol: A spiral double helix in rising smoke

Color: Blue smoke (sage burning)

Stone: Tigereye (comes alive as it moves)

Element: Air

Flower: Daisy

Herb: Sage (fresh, dried, burning)

 In the Sky, the Lord of the Dance is the North Star, around which The Heavens whirl and dance in a never-ending circle. The Twelve Winds are Birds (Dancers), each represented by a Star in one of the zodiac signs along the path of The Sun. "Thou Whirlwind" (or Woodcock) is the Thirteenth Bird, Agalu'ga, the Lead Dancer. His Place of Abode is Coma Berenices, the North Galactic Pole of the Universe. The Stars reflect the Whirligig of Life.

Wind is the Breath of The Universe, the channel of communication between Earth and Heaven. It carries Sacred Smoke up to The Great Spirit and opens the way to Universal Consciousness.

Whirlwind moves back and forth, around and about, picking up at one place, dropping off at another—the CWW (Cosmic-Wide Web) networking system.

In rhythm with the pulse of Mother Nature:

> BREATHE IN—the Cosmos pushes in.
> BREATHE OUT—the Cosmos pulls out.

Breathe out, breathe in—give and receive the Essence of The Universe.

Life begins with the first breath and ends with the last.

So the person of this Day Sign is a channel of communication, one who gathers information and circulates it.

Those of this Sign are aware of the passing panorama of life. They are mentally alert, very observant, reaching out and grasping whatever comes within the scope of their horizon. They add the spice of imagination to this fund of basic information, stirring with a big stick.

These persons are also blown about like the wind, unpredictable as the weather. They can be as swift and destructive as the tornado that cuts a swath across the prairie, making a clean sweep as with a broom, right down to ground level. Only cellar and cistern are spared. And so it is with the Whirlwind personality: reaching far and wide in breadth but not in depth.

This Sign moves in honesty and truth, as guileless and spontaneous as the wind. It is the draft of air that brings on colds and fever, then turns about and cools the fevered brow.

A breeze can be gentle and caressing, soft as a baby's breath, the whisper of a sigh, the promise of a lazy day in summer. Such is the versatility of this Sign—multifaceted as a diamond, and equally brilliant.

Wind fans embers into flame, and flames into a blazing inferno. Air is the life and breath of fire; without it the fire goes out. So the Wind Sign works through others:

It bends the tree to its will;
Its touch is the brush of a willow withe;
Its voice is the roar of thunder—
or the vibration of a guitar string;
Through the flute it sings of love and longing;
It carries the scent of roses.

Of itself, Wind is invisible—odorless, colorless, soundless. All these wonders are manifest through symbiosis with others. Which explains why these persons are more often a power behind the throne than a "King of the Mountain."

This Sign might be termed the "Silver-Tongued One." More than likely their speech is very individualistic. Their charisma depends on not only what they say but on how they say it. This is true both in the role of speaker and as a conversationalist. Both are attention-getting. This also spills over into writing, and any other form of self-expression.

Careers that appeal to those of this Sign are those that require communication skills: law, teaching, consulting, announcing, public relations, and advertising, to name a few. For these alert, expansive, freewheeling, flexible personalities have a multitude of irons in a great many fires.

Their left hand always knows what the right hand is doing, but is much too clever to blurt out any inside information. Most persons born under this Sign seem to grasp the common denominator to a great many activities, and can juggle any number of projects without dropping any. A kaleidoscope of activity that dazzles and intrigues.

A fascinating personality, open-minded, imaginative, artistic, and most obviously eclectic. Romantic and hopelessly idealistic. Fashion-conscious, but so enamored with variety that there is usually more mix than match.

Some people respond more actively to what they hear, some to what they see, and a few respond equally to both. Whirlwind people are visually accented. It's not that they don't hear well; it's only that they see even better. Physical exercise and mental exercise are both important, but not in a gymnasium. Taking long walks and hiking over hill and dale are the most appealing. The sight of buds unfurling in springtime and of leaves turning crimson in autumn trigger the imagination. A beautiful sunrise opening up a brand-new day, and a blazing sunset bringing it to a close, are equally moving.

A clump of fern fronds at the creek bank may conceal the entrance to the water monster's secret hideaway. The rocky outcrop on that hillside is sure to hold the cave of the Little People. These People can see Those People—or at least sense their presence.

These are Those who listen to Rocks and hug Trees.

Whirlwind is the Symphony of the Sacred Tree of Life, whose roots are at the North Pole, and whose trunk is the umbilical cord that connects Earth with Heaven at the North Star. From that celestial focus, the branches reach out to embrace infinity.

The unbridled bird knows freedom by soaring on the updraft.

THE SHADOW DANCE

Wind should not be a tempest-in-a-teapot type—but a full-blown twister in both physical and emotional force. The multiplicity of choices could lead to indecision and therefore failure to do anything at all. Move with the currents to take advantage of what is being offered; do not let it all pass you by. Reach out and grasp opportunities, but do not grab and hold on like a greedy child. Do not crush the fragile wings of a butterfly in heavy-handed attempts to possess it.

This Sign is likely to get on a high horse and ride off in all seven directions, following a will-o'-the-wisp, chasing a rainbow, jousting with windmills, in a quest for the impossible dream. The search for perfection leads to overload, uncertainty, self-doubt, confusion of the mind—all of which tends to drown out the small voice of reason.

Listen to the wind—it will tell you true!

HEARTH

O'YA

ᎤᏯ

Direction: West—Accent on feelings, emotions, and relationships; on personal matters of security.

Symbol: Fire in a pit in the Center

Color: Velvet black

Stone: Garnet

Element: Earth

Flower: Indian blanket

Herb: Wild ginger (heartleaf)

The Sky sign is a triangle in the constellation Orion. Its base is El Nitak (the lowest Star in Orion's Belt); and the two corners are Saiph and Rigel. The M42 nebula in the center of the triangle is the fire in the Hearth. During a world destruction by Fire, The People hid in caves under the earth—went to live with The Ant People. The Hearth was where they built a fire in the center for heat and light.

There was always a Hearth in the early log cabins; at the center of the seven-sided Council House; there is always a Fire in the Center of the Dance Ring. The Hothouse (*Osi'*) is little more than a nest of fired stones in the middle of a small enclosed mound. Fire is symbolically the Center of the Cherokee Sacred Circle, the First of the Seven Directions, the Center-of-Being to which all other directions are relative. The Cherokee Sacred Circle is comparable to the Medicine Wheel of the Plains Indians.

This Sign carries the feeling of a drumbeat in an enclosed structure, echoing back and forth from one side to the other; the pulse of a great heart beating from the very bowels of the Earth: a powerful, uncontrollable force as of earthquake, volcano, tornado, or tsunami, hidden away from the eyes of humans. It represents that phase of the Sun as it passes through the "down-under" nether regions—the Dark Side of the Sun.

Hearth is the roots of the Tree of Life—the Caldera of the True Believer, a beacon to the weary traveler. This is a person who, in the all-enveloping nothingness of night, remembers that light and life are not dead; they have only gone away for a little while. That the Sun sets in the west only to rise again in the east at the appointed hour. Everything is right there where it should be, even though it is invisible.

Hearth is The Torchbearer who holds the light and warmth that defeat Darkness. This Day Sign has the intuition to explore the labyrinthine meanderings of the mind, and probe the buried treasures of the subconscious.

A homebody, first and foremost—one who builds a house upon a rock and anchors a life on a firm foundation. A centered person with a strong territorial instinct, who draws specific boundary lines—mental, physical, and emotional. But strangely enough, this does not result in the panic of claustrophobia; this rigid seclusion gives the comfortable feeling that intruders are being fenced out rather than that they themselves are being fenced in.

This is not the Sign of a globe-trotter or of one who lives out of a suitcase or in an RV. This is a Sign whose origins are in the heart of the mountain, who never particularly cared what was on the other side.

Hearth persons have subtle ways of exerting power. They are careful to avoid the appearance of running the show; they take the attitude that their way is not just the best way, it is the only way. This is an asset for a teacher, a CEO, a leader, a healer; it is a liability in one-on-one relationships.

Hearth Signs are never afraid of hard work; they labor patiently and incessantly on long-term projects. They are very organized; once they start on a path, they look neither to the right nor to the left, but proceed in the decided direction with no thought to the need for any change. Brilliant, but not very flexible. They are inclined to stay with tried-and-true methods long after they have wrung all the life out of the old way. This very stubbornness is instrumental in bringing others around to their way of thinking. These people not only love history and tradition—they make it.

Writers of this Sign leave their footprints on the sands of time. Teachers shape the thinking of future generations. They leave a legacy that may be good or bad; radical or conservative; outdated from the past, or futuristic to impracticability—their imprint is indelible.

There is a paradox here: These people are reclusive but gregarious; they seem to know the people who are instrumental in furthering a cause. They are talkative in such areas as history and science, yet sub rosa with secrets. A Mouthpiece and a Clam. All at the same time and all wrapped up in the same-sized package, with no frills—not likely to be tied with a ribbon—just stamped with their own official seal.

Hearth Signs show respect for their parents, for their ancestors, and for the past in general. They honor not only the traditions of the elders but also current civic rota. And although they have this deep-seated passion for ritual, they do not flaunt their own feelings in public. There is no weeping and wailing and gnashing of teeth for the pure joy of dramatic impact. Much like the Masked Dancers in some of the olde-time Ceremonies, their countenance masks their inner feelings for the most part. They take a stand and hold fast to it. Like a rock—a marble statue with a Mona Lisa smile.

Ritual magic is an attempt to control nature in daily life. For example, folk magic is a belief that if you want something to be true, you should act in all ways as if it is already true. If you believe strong enough and long enough, the surrounding elements will become entrained to your rhythm and all resistance will fall away. This would appear to hold the secret of success for people of this Sign.

Fire is The Sun Spirit's alter ego on earth, and the Hearth is Her Altar. Persons of this Sign are usually the Center, the Core, the very Pulse of The People.

THE SHADOW DANCE

Balance the Earth is the great secret of life. Find a comfortable middle road between bulldog tenacity and mulish obstinacy—between groovy and settled in a rut. Don't let fear of failure slow you down; anyone who appears to be right *all* the time gets a little tiresome. But never put your faith in gambling or double-dealing to stimulate cash flow.

You may be afflicted with intellectual rigidity, a tendency to be over-logical to the point of picayunishness, a desire to dominate every situation, and just plain ole ornery stubbornness. There is danger of becoming frozen in one place; if you don't learn to bend, you will surely break.

This Sign is more a loner than a team player. Although very adept at giving instructions, you find it hard to follow orders.

Always within the realm of reason, loosen up every now and then and try something new, just for the fun of it.

DRAGON

UKTE'NA

ᎤᏍᏗᎾ

Direction: South—Summer, sociability, warmth, and abundance; fruitfulness; dancing with the Moon.

Symbol: Dragon with one crystal eye

Color: Saffron (orange-yellow)

Stone: Quartz crystal

Element: Fire

Flower: Fireweed (willow herb)

Herb: Dragon's tongue (spotted wintergreen)

 This Sign is represented in the Sky by the constellation Draco, winding its way between the Little Dipper and the Big Dipper. Since about 3000 b.c. Polaris has possessed the Magic Crystal (North Star). Eventually the Dragon will recapture it, and the North Star will again be Thuban, a bright yellow Star in Draco. The Dragon represents Matriarchy, the Great Mother figure, as distinguished from Patriarchy, the Masculine or Father principle. The North Star is passed around in a circle up there in the Sky as the Worlds turn in a cycle down here below.

Dragon is the Corn Spirit, personification of the dual personality of Corn Mother and Corn Maiden. This is a Sign of fertility and procreation from generation to generation. The entire Corn plant, on her earth-skirt mound, appears as the Mother, holding in her arms a ripened ear of corn—her daughter. The babe is snugly wrapped in corn shucks. A veritable Madonna and Child.

In the Beginning, cornmeal was moistened with saliva and shaped into human form, both male and female; that's the Story of Creation (and Re-Creation). Corn has ever been the sacred manna of The People. When trotting along the trail from dawn to dusk for many suns, the Traveler carried nothing to eat along the way but parched corn.

The very word *dragon* means "eye, to look at, to see clearly"—as of the reputed mother who has "eyes in the back of her head." She seems to see everything everywhere, past, present, and future, much like the *Ulunsu'ti* Stone, the crystal eye of *Ukte'na*, the mythical Cherokee monster.

The Dragon breathes fire, is touchy and jealous of her authority, easily roused to violence. This woman cracks a mean whip: when she yells "Frog!" everyone is expected to jump. The Dragon Spirit has ever been known as The Lawgiver, The Judge, a Dispenser of Justice—one who "lays down the law!"

She is a veritable old battle-ax in defense of her family and loved ones. Vigilant and protective, a champion of their causes, loyal even unto death itself.

These qualities are equally true of the male of the Sign, who becomes a father figure. He is a taskmaster, demanding perfection of his sons. Daughters are compelled to obedience; they are only expected to toe a different line. And of course no young man alive is good enough to marry his daughter.

According to geomancy, there are ley lines of energy or magnetic force all over the Earth. The Chinese call them Dragon lines, and they are divided into yin and yang. The yin, or feminine, Dragon lines are in the valleys; the yang, or masculine, Dragon lines are in the mountains.

This energy, sometimes called orgone energy, pyramid power, or animal magnetism, can be collected and actually put to use. The Hopi Kiva is a collection chamber for orgone energy. The Great Pyramid of Egypt, as well as the Mayan pyramids, are also collection centers for Dragon power, as are the vortexes at Sedona, Arizona. These places are believed to be very healthy—to recharge the batteries of humans in the same manner as electrical batteries are recharged.

The yang Dragon lines in the mountains include the great volcanoes that erupt when there is power overload. Storms and earthquakes are also triggered by this Dragon power. Where the yin and yang lines intersect are the most powerful spots. This is where the Native American Medicine Wheels and the pagan dance circles are located; cathedrals have been built on these same sacred sites, right on top of the sacred circles of olden times.

Dragons churn up the elements, sail with the winds, and frolic with the waves. They are more than mortal, delightfully devilish, and also divine. They light up the darkness with the torch of their fiery breath; they root out the seeds of pestilence, effecting purification by fire.

Dragons are collectors of bright and beautiful things. They

hoard valuables. Greek myth has it that a Dragon was set to guard the apples of the Hesperides, the fruit of knowledge and eternal life. Certainly Draco encircles the North Star, the tip of the Heavenly Tree of Life.

Such is the personality of the Dragon Day Sign: one who beats a path here and there and everywhere, stirring things with a big stick.

Persons of this Sign are unique characters, aggressive and domineering, truly unpredictable: crafty and full of strong emotions, wily as a fox, ornery as any coyote, and irrepressible as a juvenile delinquent.

A remark just in passing: The Babylonian monster Dragon, Tiamat, who was the chaos of the Primeval Waters, was said to be invincible as long as she kept her mouth shut; the Dragon-Slayer was able to destroy her only when she opened it.

The Dragon Sign is the spirit of uninhibited gaiety and flamboyant sexuality, generated by the rhythmic energy of the Dance. This Cherokee Dance Ritual is a caressing of the Earth, which pushes aside the mask from the mystery of creation. The drumbeat is one great heartbeat, connecting the End to the new Beginning in the Sacred Circle of Life.

Dragons are the most widespread and oldest mythical beasts in history, combining wisdom, insight, and the divine vision of change. An ancient symbol of good luck, this Sign is the cornucopia of abundance—blessed with a rich and satisfying life.

THE SHADOW DANCE

Persons of this Sign may become too involved in their own interests, too set in their ways, and lack the mental mobility to break out of the shell of the patterns of the past.

On the other hand, in addition to their generally good-natured charm, they are jealous, impatient victims of up-and-down mood swings; they seesaw between rash overenthusiasm for new fads and falling back into the same old rut. Lack of initiative can create a "lounge lizard."

This "on-again, off-again" emotional hangup may be reflected in their sex lives, often spilling over into erotic fantasy and deviance— at best into strangeness. Or total suppression, which is equally destructive.

This type is apt to be frantically interested in a multitude of extremes, like the knight who jumped on his horse and rode off in all seven directions.

Balance is the secret of success in this Sign. Don't fly too high nor dig too deep; don't color too far outside the lines—beyond which are Dragons!

SERPENT

DO TSI

V K

Direction: East—The accent is on emergence of the individual personality; internal strength and ability.

Symbol: Serpent

Color: Red flame

Stone: Fire opal

Element: Water

Flower: Passionflower (maypop)

Herb: Green and red peppers

 In the Sky, the Serpent is the constellation Serpens, along the Milky Way (The River) from the *Agwan'ti* Tree (of knowledge), Northern Cross (Cygnus). Serpent People are reputed to be the Sky People who come to Earth periodically as Educators when The People have turned away from knowledge: ETs landing in UFOs.

> Rainbow is the tongue
> of the Celestial Serpent,
> flicking off the rain.

As above, so below: on Earth the Serpent was at the roots of the Tree of Knowledge in the Garden of Eden. And in the human body the coiled Serpent power is found at the base chakra, the taut spring that energizes the human body—all the way up the spine (tree), right up through the crown chakra; and from there out and straight up to merge with the energy of the Sun.

The Serpent power is the vital energy, the moving force, the instinct and desire for creativity, the trigger that sets off the action. It lights the fuse that explodes and magnifies the life force itself. This includes not only sexual energy but also love, passion, hate, goodness, meanness, and compassion.

Serpent types are intellectuals; they have high IQs and usually keep abreast of what is happening in the world. They often take up mental pursuits, science, technology, or psychology. They sometimes become so overloaded with theory that they need therapy themselves.

The Serpent Sign intensifies not only the life force but also its dual polarity, the death force. Either they have more brushes with death than usual, or they are more caught up in emotional reactions to the death of a loved one. It is important that this Day Sign understand that death is as much a part of the scheme of things as life, and that it must be accepted.

This Sign emits strong emotional waves, both positive and negative. This is one who loves very deeply and hates with a passion.

The fires of the Serpent power burn fiercely and can either purify for the good of all, or burn to ashes to the wanton destruction of all things. In this Sign are the fertile seeds of both life and death.

Two Serpents twined about the winged staff comprise the symbol of healing, the caduceus. These two are representative of healing and oracular ability. Strangely enough, in the distant past the magician was also the physician. Not so strange when you consider that psychoanalysis and medicine go hand in hand in present-day healing.

The Rattle, symbolic of the rattle of the Rattlesnake, was commonly used in Cherokee healing practice, as was the Rattlesnake Tooth for scratching before applying the herbal liquids. The Serpent Sign is the symbol of healing.

In legend the Serpent led The People out of the Cave of Darkness and into the Sunlight of knowledge and intelligence.

The Serpent is probably the oldest and most widely recognized symbol of the masculine principle of the universe—a phallic symbol par excellence. American Indians set great store in the ceremony of the Medicine Man, which bestowed Serpent Bravery upon the warriors as they went into battle, to assure their invincibility.

Serpent Day Sign types are not only strong-willed but also charismatic personalities. Others are very aware of them, but never seem to know them at all—they give off an unpretentious air of mystery. They have sex appeal; they take center stage and know how to hold attention. They have a dramatic flair, and sometimes are still in performance long after the final curtain has been lowered and the stagehands are striking the set.

They have strong emotions, and strong opinions that vibrate those around them like the thwang of a violin string. There is a tendency to become fanatical on a pet subject. They sometimes create fear and awe, a feeling of primitive man with a club, throwing a woman over his shoulder and carrying her off to his cave.

Leadership comes naturally to those of this Day Sign, for they seem to know how to attract attention, and how to gather followers. They naturally gravitate to the spotlight, yet they have an aura of mystery; persons that everybody knows, but nobody really understands. Their personality is difficult to describe accurately. Sometimes they become so charged up that they may be seen as accidents running around looking for a place to happen!

The Serpent is an ancient Spirit of Resurrection. Because he often changes his skin, he appears to be reborn over and over again. Each new skin is necessary because of continual growth. This is observed as a sloughing off of the old to make room for the new, which is a very good thing, if it isn't carried too far.

The Serpent is carnivorous and lives in the ground, in his own secret, solitary lair, coming out only when his extroverted personality traits come to the surface.

The Serpent is associated with springs and groundwater, with storms and the wrath of Mother Nature, whirlpools, the violence of youth and "deathless" young love; the temporary, breathtaking beauty of nature, with its ensuing death and destruction; renewal and rebirth in the never-ending cycle of life itself.

The Serpent has been much maligned, perhaps most famously in the Garden of Eden story. But in truth, Adam and Eve were deteriorating in Eden. A "no-conflict" situation was making them soft. The Serpent opened their eyes to understanding. Stirred things around with a big stick. Threw them out into the real world where they would live and learn and grow stronger—become aware of truth—not live in a pleasant stupor in the perfect garden.

Serpent awakened their consciousness.

THE SHADOW DANCE

The Serpent type has a tendency to fall in love with his own voice, and his own body, and suffers the delusion that these physical attributes are the true Entity (the Soul). Maintaining a delicate balance between the Dual Polarities of the Universe (Night and Day, Love and Hate, and so forth) is particularly important.

When the volcano of this personality is about to erupt, some turn to alcohol as a form of release, which is the path to destruction. (When you feel driven, don't drink!)

Slough off the old, outgrown skin of the past to make room for the new and innovative ideas that are your stock in trade. Come out of the cave of darkness into the sunlight of freedom.

Serpent Sign people have the ability to live and function under near-impossible duress, but may have trouble knowing when enough is enough. There is a tendency to fall into the rut of routine, of what others dictate to be the "right" way to go.

TWINS

TAKATO'KA

W S V S

Direction: North—Storm center; place of wisdom and purification; power of renewal; hour of midnight.

Symbol: Handfasting infinity sign

Color: Dove gray (white and black)

Stone: Onyx (agate)

Element: Air

Flower: Honeysuckle

Herb: Willow

The Twins of first import in the Sky are the female Sun and the male Moon, whose union keeps the world going round in perpetuity. But since Cherokee myth has it that the Morning Star appeared first to herald the coming of The Sun, Venus—as both Morning Star and Evening Star—represents the twins. Other noted pairs are Castor and Pollux (Flint and Reed), Sirius and Antares (the Dog Stars), and Pleiades and Hyades (Star Clusters in Taurus). Dual Polarities (Twins) appear throughout the Universe.

Those brought into the world under this Sign are subject to major changes all along the way: alienation from family, marriage and divorce, running the gauntlet in the workplace. They ride tsunamis of earthquake and upheaval, proclaim indisputable verities, make their own waves wherever they go. They find it hard to follow the straight and narrow; easier to hold center stage with dynamics. They undergo powerful transformations: death and resurrection alternate like a flashing neon sign.

There is an ongoing challenge to Balance the Earth—like the seesaw on a children's playground, which moves up and down easily when the two ends carry equal weight. (We called it a teeter-totter when I was a child, but that was a long, long time ago.) If too much weight (or importance) is placed on one end, then the whole thing gets bogged down and won't work at all. The two ends of a seesaw compare to the opposites of the Universe. They are The Twins, the mirror images of each other; they go together but, like unruly children, they just won't behave.

Some examples of these opposites are: Night and Day, Positive and Negative, Leader and Follower, Joy and Sorrow, War and Peace, Pride and Modesty, Love and Hate, Male and Female.

This Sign will be faced throughout life with the deep midnight darkness of indecision; it's an ongoing dilemma. Too much, too soon is as bad as too little, too late. To be good but not too good. To understand where bravery ends and foolhardiness begins.

This is the Sign of an idealist who still believes in knights in shining armor and diamond tiaras. In the pot of gold at the end of the rainbow. Reach for them; they are there for the taking! All the glitter and glamor of the beautiful people will be showered upon those who truly seek them.

Enjoy your possessions as long as you own them. When they own you, throw the rascals out. Don't hold on too tight for too long.

An indisputable verity of life is that for every action there is an equal and opposite reaction. Theoretically, yes; but in actual fact, not so. There is a tendency to bicker over nonsense. Two and two may add up to four in mathematics, but in chemistry the same equation can blow you right out of the arena. Your faith is the canoe that you paddle safely through the troubled waters of life. Fill your day with all reasonable effort—then go to bed and let the stars work their magic. For there is still magic in the world! Follow your Guiding Star.

Persons of the Sign may get so caught up in cause and effect that they miss out on the magic altogether. When the glass slipper is offered, put it on and wear it; if you waste time rationalizing about it, the party's over and the lights are out before you even get to dance.

This is the Sign of an overachiever who keeps on fighting long after the battle is won. He rows upstream against the current instead of gliding along like a graceful swan, leaving a wake of gentle ripples. It is not enough that he has won the prize; he must drive every single nail into place to set the record straight. Right is right and wrong is wrong; battle lines must be drawn and must be resolved before the slate can be cleared.

There is a strong urge toward community service. Those born under this Sign believe that everyone is entitled to food, shelter, and clothing, and that the favored few who enjoy these essentials have a responsibility to see that other, less fortunate ones are provided for. They will sacrifice time from their own busy schedules to help others. They hold to tradition, conforming to social rules of behavior set out by the masses, while at the same time flaunting the very act of breaking some of these same rules. There is a fierce desire to be different—to express flamboyant individuality. There is that Lady-of-the-Manor arrogance expressed by showing how absolutely down-to-earth they can afford to be. It is a matter of following the letter of the law, whether that laid down by society at large or by their own dictates.

This Sign is stimulated by the challenge of danger, the thrill of walking through the valley of the shadow of death in order to experience the exhilaration of the climb to the mountaintop. Riding a motorcycle or making a parachute jump is exciting; it never occurs to this personality that Lady Luck may be looking the other way, letting disaster crash through.

Twin is a mirrored image appearing in reverse, and veiled in swirling dove-gray smoke—the same smoke that carries messages from Earthlings to The Great Spirit . . . .

It is an echo of the human voice, resounding in Thunder and Wind . . . .
It is the Beginning and the End and everything in between . . . .
It is all there is, was, or ever will be in Heaven and Earth.
It is INFINITY.

THE SHADOW DANCE

The Twin type has a tendency to hold on to things long after they have outlived their usefulness, and to hold on to people when all the compatibility has worn off. Don't hold on too tight for too long. When it's over, it's over. There is a problem of refusing to accept the fact that you cannot make people over. You can't win 'em all!

There is a difference between bulldog tenacity and mulish obstinacy. Close the door to the old, worn-out past; forget it. Let go; surrender; release—and forgive. Throw off the old dead husks that hold you down, and rise, free and strong, to even greater heights. Brush away any cobwebs that entangle you. There are mountains to climb and rivers to cross; places to go and things to do. But remember that when you reach the top of the mountain there is no place to go but down; and when you hit the bottom of the bucket there is no way to go but up. Keep your eyes on wonderful, magical happenings; you will miss them altogether if you're busy feeling sorry for yourself.

Your creativity thrives on harmony and with conflict, but only with manageable amounts of each.

DEER

AHWU'SDI

D Ꮎ Ꮝ Ꭵ

Direction: West—Where the Wind blows free; sensitivity; compromise in relations with others, away from an accent on self.

Symbol: Stag

Color: Tawny beige

Stone: Turquoise

Element: Earth

Flower: Deer eye (black-eyed Susan)

Herb: Rabbit tobacco (life everlasting)

 In the Sky this Sign is represented by the constellation Galagina, the Stag—otherwise known as Taurus, the Bull. It does not include the Pleiades and Hyades Star Clusters, which were seen as separate constellations by the Cherokee. The Great Horned Sky Rabbit originally owned those beautiful horns but lost them to the Stag in a game of chance—a long, long time ago.

Deer are part of Mother Nature's overall plan to feed The People. The first wave in the food chain is plant life: fruit, seeds, bark, leaves, and grass. Deer eat this plant life, creating a second wave in the food supply that swells to a tsunami of superabundance. The Cherokee philosophy is that Animals are our brothers; it is the purpose of their existence to feed mankind. To refuse to eat meat is to deny our brothers their destiny, their very reason for being.

And thus it is with persons of this Sign: they are gatherers of food and supplies; they enjoy rituals, banquets, feasts, and ceremonials; they are charitable and giving, lighthearted and spontaneous, dispensers of hospitality, the soul of sociability.

These champions of good sportsmanship are at home in the forest: walkers, runners, hunters—equally adept with gun or camera. Like the Deer in the myth of the Ball Game who could outrun every other animal, they are lithe and lively, able to cover a lot of territory in a short time, even allowing time to pronk and play along the way.

In myth, Deer and Rabbit are gregarious companions who match brain and brawn in competitive play.

The Roman myth of Romulus and Remus, who were suckled by a Wolf, finds its counterpart in a Cherokee myth of the Mother Doe nurturing a baby girl who became the Great Mother of *Anikahwi'*, the Deer Clan. And the Spirit Little Deer, *Ahwu'sdi*, watches over all the earthly deer (as distinguished from the big spirit animals in the Sky). She is always immediately at hand to see if each hunter asks pardon before killing a deer; if not, she tracks him down and afflicts him with crippling rheumatism.

In Cherokee thought there is no essential difference between humans and animals; in the distant past they lived and worked together in harmony, until man became so overbearing and heedless of the rights of others that the animals turned against him.

And so it is with Deer Sign persons: Though basically gentle and peace-loving, they are quick to speak up for what they know is right. They never hesitate to step boldly into any confrontation with those who infringe on their territory, or who trample on the rights of others. They are concerned with family and social integrity; they have an urge to set things right. This tends to upset the apple cart and result in turbulent and frustrating relationships.

But for the most part, this Sign practices passive domination, a kind of "iron fist in a velvet glove" philosophy. Here is one who just never seems to understand any other way than their own way, who acts as if that is how things are, were, and are going to be—a kind of folk magic that is remarkably effective over the long haul.

The masculine characteristics of Deer come out at the mating season. A Stag in rut is equated, in one of the sacred formulas, with a Storm, the force behind wind, clouds, rain, thunder, and lightning, raging up and down the mountainside, tossing and trampling everything in his path. Horns are a universal symbol of virility. The growth of antlers in the rainy season (all forms of water are masculine) corresponds to his aggressiveness. His antlers drop off in the hot, dry season (Sun and Fire are feminine), and with them goes the compulsive competitive urge.

So goes the human cycle of storm alternating with fair weather for this Sign; it is not so easy to tell what triggers these mood changes—possibly a swing between physical and spiritual. For this Sign is in a sense indicative of the Beginning and the End: a gateway between one state of existence and another. This means change.

Beneath the surface these personalities struggle with freedom versus security issues. They often leave home at an early age to establish their own independent lives. However, family ties are rarely severed. There is ever an urge to take off for parts unknown, possibly to relocate, along with the desire for the security of home and family. The struggle with this conflict leads them to unique solutions; they often become innovators of somewhat unconventional personal lifestyles. Frequently, they have unusual interests that are of an investigative or searching nature. They are known for breaking the rules peacefully out of necessity.

Whatever the inner turmoil, this Sign is always aware of what is going on roundabout, and alert to opportunities that arise. This includes a fine-honed sense of difficulties and dangers.

Persons of this Sign are artistic and inspiring. They are inclined to dabble in the arts: writing, painting, music. Although ready to fight for the rights of others, they have a supersensitivity that imposes a reluctance to bare their own souls for critical review.

Deer Sign is in harmony with the lunar cycles, awake and active all night when the Moon is full. A personification of beauty, a graceful sinuous dancer tuned to the rhythm of the Earth, activated by the energy of the Sun. Who gathers the flowers of the Universe into a *Gadug'*, The People's granary, an olde-time Cherokee system for nourishing the Seven Clans (the world, that is).

THE SHADOW DANCE

Do not confuse the tools you gather about you with what is doing the work. The tool is not the power; the power is you and the light that flows through you. Darkness is only the absence of light; let the light shine through. Lighten up your life; develop a sense of humor; enjoy laughter, it's good for anything that ails you. There is a danger of inflexibility; don't fall into a rut; be on the lookout for change and take advantage of it. There is the issue of completing things; taking on too much creates problems of feeling pressured or scattered. And procrastination is destructive.

The ebb and flow of life is not just one step forward and two steps back. It's the enjoyable rhythm of the dance of the Cosmos— you have only to get in step. The trick is not to hang on too long nor to give up too soon. Swing and sway all along the way, and stop to smell those flowers as you gather them. Remember that the joy is in climbing up the mountain; when you get to the top there is nowhere to go but down.

RABBIT

NOQUI'SEGWA'

Ꮓ ꮘꮞꮖ

Direction: South—Summertime and high noon; fruitfulness; flitting butterflies and flowers. Outspoken, emotional.

Symbol: Rabbit

Color: Brass

Stone: Emerald

Element: Fire

Flower: Prairie wild rose

Herb: Catbrier

 The Great Horned Sky Rabbit is the planet Venus, The Great Star or Morning Star. The Cherokee Sacred Calendar is a Venus Calendar of 260 days (20 Day Signs × 13 Numbers). Although Venus orbits the Sun every 584 days (as seen from Earth), it appears as the Morning Star for a little over 260 days, and as the Evening Star a little more than 260 days; which is also the gestation time of the human fetus. Next to the Sun and the Moon, Venus was the most carefully observed portent in the Sky. It has crescent horns, and casts a shadow.

Rabbit is the Trickster of Cherokee culture, the role that Coyote plays in most Native American stories. He is the Br'er Rabbit of African folktales, which either originated with or are contemporaries of Cherokee folktales of the same mischievous rascal. Throughout the world the Hare, along with the Cat, is the most likely candidate for a Witch's familiar; Hare has ever been known as a chameleon-like sleight-of-hand artist who wears the hat of a great many personalities.

He is the politician who tells his constituents whatever they are waiting to hear; the big wheeler-dealer medicine show barker who peddles tonic elixir of youth in a bottle (and at the very reasonable price of only a dollar). He is, in fact, the Messenger par excellence who carries information to the far corners of the Earth. He doesn't always get the details right, but for such an entertaining fellow the welcome mat is always out.

Rabbit is the personification of Light and New Life, Sunrise: Lord of the Dawn. His Twin Brother was Flint, Shadow of the West, Sunset: Lord of Darkness. The war between them was long and dreadful; bitter battles raged from east to west, back and forth, as the sparks flew outward. Rabbit finally outsmarted Flint: fed him a big dinner and afterward, when Flint fell asleep, drove a wooden stake through his heart. The pieces of Flint flew all over the Earth; one hit Rabbit on the mouth, creating his "harelip."

Over most of North America, particularly in Mexico and east of the Mississippi, the Great White Rabbit was a cultural hero as well as a trickster. Many of the Rabbit tales were incorporated in Longfellow's epic poem of the legendary Iroquoian chief, Hiawatha, whose most important contributions to mankind were fire and tobacco. Rabbit brought these back from his journeys for the use of his grandmother, Earth, and himself. The Sacred tobacco was to be used for communication with the spirits—never to be abused as a recreational drug. Fire, probably the greatest boon to mankind on Earth, can be even more destructive if allowed to get out of hand.

Queen Boadicea, who revolted against the Roman occupation of Britain, carried the moon hare on her banner. The moon hare was also dedicated to the Saxon goddess Eostre at her rites of spring. Irish peasants still observe the matriarchal taboo on eating the flesh of the hare, because it is totemic. The Easter Bunny, along with the egg, colored red to proclaim new birth, has carried over to the present day. Easter is the time of resurrection, the pregnant phase of the flowering of the Earth.

White Rabbit is alive and well in our current literature in *Alice in Wonderland;* Harvey is the whimsical Rabbit of stage and film. The loveable rascal Bugs Bunny is now on a U.S. postal stamp.

In Cherokee mythology "the man in the moon" is the father of all children on Earth; in this matrilineal society, bloodlines were traced only through the mother. Sky Rabbit is a scion of Moon, the fertility symbol, an innate response to the invitation: Be fruitful and multiply.

Rabbit was also the Leader of The Dance, and the basic function of The Dance is to Balance the Earth. This, too, is incorporated into the personality of this Day Sign. The humor and foolishness point out what's wrong as well as what's right in the overall behavior of The People, a very effective form of communication.

Rabbit is able to turn his head to see 360 degrees—all the way around. This sign is able to see all the sides of any question, and therefore may have trouble reaching a decision—even when he does he is apt to change his mind from time to time.

It was the Sky Rabbit who told The People of the coming of the Pleiades Star Cluster, with their warning of the Flood that would cover all; he gathered them in the arc of his crescent horns and carried them over the waves until the water receded and there was again dry land. He told them of the coming of the Sun, bringing with it a bright New World. He then gathered together all the leftovers from the Flood and Re-Created the population of the Earth.

Rabbit and Deer were always good friends who matched wits and engaged in competitive sports for the entertainment of the spectators. Rabbit was a habitual gambler; he lost his horns to Deer in a game of chance. He often lost his shirt in such games, but it never seemed to present a problem: he could talk his way out of almost any situation.

Rabbit is a Discoverer, a Way Show-er, a hero with a thousand faces; also a tricky type with an excess of nervous energy and a need for attention. One who enjoys dropping a bone of contention into any group just to raise an atmosphere of excitement.

But whatever his trespasses, this one is always forgiven. He represents those desirable qualities that are so often suppressed in the human creature: softness, gentleness, and vulnerability—a beloved "warm fuzzy" in an otherwise cold, cruel world.

THE SHADOW DANCE

Although Rabbit is alert, quick, and moves rapidly, especially when startled, he is known to run willy-nilly in erratic patterns. He may work tirelessly on a project that is quite useless, even if it never reaches a conclusion. In negotiating those big deals, he usually resorts to drinking, and could easily end up an alcoholic. He might express unpopular opinions simply to stimulate argumentation and debate. Excess nervous energy could lead to risk-taking, which ends up in self-destruction.

This Sign succeeds more often as an employee rather than as the boss, for although he appears to be aggressively overconfident, he is likely to be basically insecure. He is more successful at major projects if the responsibilities are shared; he needs to have his confidence bolstered along the way. Here is a great starter, full of earth-shaking ideas—but a poor finisher, who loses steam long before the home stretch. As in the fable of the race between the Hare and the Tortoise.

THE RIVER

YUN·WI GUNNAHI·TA

Ᏸ Ꮻ ᎬᎾᎭᏫ

Direction: East—Awakening, creativity; the Third Eye; strong feelings and emotions.

Symbol: Winding river

Color: Iridescence

Stone: Rainbow crystal (quartz)

Element: Water

Flower: Trillium

Herb: Cattail

 On Earth it is The River of Life and in the sky it is The River of Death, or The Path of Souls—The Milky Way. As above, so below, for in Cherokee philosophy every single thing down here on Earth is but a shadow of that which appears in the Sky. The Milky Way is *Gihli' Utsun'stanun'yi* "Where the Dog Ran," for the Spirit Dog Star gathers souls to the Heavens. The River is a minion of Grandfather Moon.

Long Man (*Yun'wi Gunnahi'ta*) is the sacred personification of The River, whose head lies at the top of the mountain, whose feet are in the lowlands, and whose body stretches all along the way in between. He is ever speaking to those who will listen and can understand.

Persons of this Sign have wonderful imaginations and find "sermons in stones, and good in everything." They live in a world peopled with Fairies, Leprechauns, and Little People. All things great and wonderful are their forte. They can easily be psychic, if they only put their minds to it.

Quite often these people are successful performers—artists, writers, musicians, magicians. They may run with the beautiful people or follow romantic lifestyles. There is an underlying need for public recognition, and this can be satisfied through any number of channels. But wherever this one marches, it is to a different drummer, vibrating colors and rhythms straight from the soul, driven by volcanic inner forces that are unknown to the rest of us. This enigmatic Sign is a mystery to the masses.

River Signs can easily be overwhelmed by their own emotional overflow, generating violent reactions within themselves. They also arouse others to extreme actions—dominating those in their circle of influence. They are strong, independent thinkers who are sometimes capable and perfectly willing to solve all their problems entirely on their own; however, this is necessarily difficult, because they have a habit of getting in over their heads. By nature they take responsibilities very seriously, and are always in danger of getting bogged down in a metaphysical maze. When they have been apprenticed to good role models, they take responsibility and leadership in stride.

These people have a natural flair for grandstanding, which can be both a blessing and a curse. When luck is with them, they can bulldoze their way right up to the top; when fortune frowns, they get caught up in the stagnant backwash of destructive lifestyles. A deep-seated inferiority complex sometimes activates this obsession for recognition. Unfortunately, such unhealthy action sets a bad example for their followers, who find defiance to be charismatic and sexy.

This Sign is a risk-taker; too often he will go for broke and lead others to follow suit; with missionary zeal he picks up everything along the way and lulls it to quiescence, to go with the flow. Just like The River, who gathers in and carries away.

Natural-born leaders of this Day Sign have a dream, and they are willing to spend their lives bringing it to reality. They have purpose and drive that is above and beyond the call of duty. Theirs is an uncompromising conviction that there is only one true way— their way. No halfway measures, it is all or nothing—and that attitude itself is often the key to success in any undertaking. If they can learn to accept responsibility for their own actions and decisions, there is no limit to the heights they may reach.

However, the elusive prize is not always worth the struggle. This person may be hitching his wagon to the Star of the Archangel, Michael—or he may be following the Archfiend, Lucifer, on a collision course, right down to the bottom of the bucket! The fire of each burns equally bright, and beckons with the same intensity. The ability to separate the seed from the chaff is the key.

Water is plastic and changeable as a chameleon. It takes the shape of any vessel that will contain it; the boundaries determine the form. It can be solid, liquid, or gas—possibly the most malleable element in the Universe, the most prolific, and the most vital. It is adaptable to any space or form, and very soluble in almost anything; it is colorless, odorless, and tasteless. Such versatility is nothing short of mind-boggling. When channeled and directed, it can work miracles!

This Sign will usually receive full recognition for all accomplishments, both good and bad. He gets carried along by his own momentum to the very end of the line. His is the "hot line" to the Universal Consciousness—he need only listen in.

The River Sign includes storm, rain, raindrop—and teardrop. There is vibration to all the sin, sorrow, suffering, and sadness that prevails; there is a desire to smooth the rocky road for fellow travelers; and there is a recurring cycle of the return of the Master Teachers who will awaken the world to the Brotherhood of Man, the Great White Light, Duyugdun, "It is right!"

Moonlight on The River sparks the fires of creativity—Moon and Water are the masculine fundaments that fertilize Mother Earth.

THE RIVER is The Fountain of Life.

THE SHADOW DANCE

There is a constant need to strive for control of violent passions, to seek mature counsel, and to stay well within the boundaries of the channel of life. There is a tendency to blame it on the system when things go wrong. The greatest challenge is to take responsibility for mistakes as well as successes that occur along the way.

You must learn to discipline yourself, or you will have to accept the discipline of others. Primitive, uncontrolled drives translate negatively into misuse of power, sexual perversion, alcoholism, substance abuse, and failure. Wash out all negative thoughts; let them flow away down the stream.

Harness the dynamic power that is within you; shape it to your will. Remember that the whole world was once destroyed by Flood—which is only The River out of control.

WOLF

KANATI

ᎠᎾᏟ

Direction: North—Wisdom; creative mind within the traditions of the group; purification—the rigors of cold and storm.

Symbol: Wolf

Color: Sable brown

Stone: Obsidian

Element: Air

Flower: Bluebonnet

Herb: Flowering dogwood

Symbols in the Sky are Sirius, at one end of the Milky Way (The Path of Souls) where it touches the horizon, and Antares on the other end. One or the other is always visible, but never both at the same time. When the Soul enters The Way, it crosses over a raging river on a log. Only the brave get across; the weak fall into the torrent below. Agise'gwa, the Great Female (Sirius), and Wa'hyaya', the Alpha Male (Antares), must both be fed, or they will not allow the Soul to pass. It is possible to get caught between the two, and wander endlessly back and forth across that Great River in the Sky.

Wolf is our Brother; he shares our very roots; he goes back to the time before memory. All dogs are domesticated wolves—this was accomplished so very long ago that our legends of companionship and guidance often refer to a tame wolf—the dog.

But this wild, feral creature who sings to high heaven when the Moon is full is kana'ti, the Lucky Hunter, the real Wolf, minion of Moon and Man along that last stretch of darkness before the resurrection of light: the Hour of the Wolf—a Time of Birth and of Death—that borderline between night and dawn.

For Wolf is a connecting link between the dark of the Otherworld and the light of everyday existence; a psychic doorway between two worlds. Although a Medicine Woman or Man is more likely to have Rattlesnake Tooth for a Natal Day Sign, the Spirit Guide or "familiar" of that Medicine Person is popularly a Wolf. Long before central heating and electric blankets were invented, the domesticated wolf was called into service as an animated incubator to keep the patients warm. One of the medicinal magic formulas calls on this spirit to cure frostbite, because his paw pads are believed to be "frost-free." Wearing the mask, fur tail, paws, and claws of Wolf proclaims the area of expertise of the *Ada'wehi:* Healer.

On the other hand, a dispenser of magic charms and love potions—a conjuror—might be calling on Grandmother Spider for assistance.

Wolf is a two-way personality—genial to his own kind, but savagely protective against all outsiders. Lover of freedom and the wide open spaces. A "don't fence me in" character. The paradox here is that he marks his own territory aggressively, fencing others out!

Wolf is patriarchal—believes in the double standard: one set of rules for the behavior of males and quite another for females. There is an established pecking order wherein the Alpha Male Wolf is top dog! The Alpha Female Wolf is the top position of all females. Each member knows his place in the hierarchy; those who rebel are ousted and forced to form their own pack or live as lone wolves.

Only the Alpha pair are permitted to have puppies. The entire pack cooperates to feed and care for the little ones. And to enjoy them. These are very social animals; they hunt together, bring food back to the den and eat together with the puppies, which they carry about clamped in jaws that are lined with needle-sharp teeth. The ancient folklore that tells of a Wolf who nursed the twin founders of Rome has captured the imagination of all ages; the tale is as timeless as the eternal city itself. Not only the parents but all the members of the pack are nurturers.

There is a general atmosphere of friendly playfulness in the pack; they gather on moonlit nights for choral howling that echoes back and forth from mountaintop to mountaintop. This is a form of bonding as well as communication with friends and relatives who are temporarily separated. All bay to Grandfather Moon, and howl and bark for the love of the sound of their own voices. A kind of bow-wow powwow!

This Day Sign symbolizes activity and movement, as well as passage between physical and spiritual planes; a sanguine patrol of the home ground and all surrounding neighborhoods. Not to be confused with wanderlust; more like taking care of business on the home front.

Here is a Trailblazer who guides Travelers through the labyrinthine ways of this world and the next; a Navigator through uncharted waters, who senses exactly where he is going, even if he has never been there before. It is the Sign of a courageous and generous personality who is primed for deeds of derring-do, like a stick of dynamite with a short fuse. He will ski with the avalanche, save the damsel in distress, brave the caldera of the volcano, and smoke the Dragon out. A generous provider who will share his worldly goods as well as his ideas with the poorest comer. Prodigal of possessions, as if the abundance of the Earth were boundless. All this alone to be helpful.

A Wolf personality is one who may be very successful running his own business; he knows how to inspire the loyalty of employees because he is comfortable in that atmosphere. Strangely enough, he is also an excellent member of the team, for he understands the strength of pulling together and the necessity of starting at the bottom and working all the way up.

Diplomacy goes hand in hand with a sense of humor in this Sign. Subtlety and tact oil the machinery of cooperative endeavor at all levels. A court jester may play the fool, but he is forgiven a multitude of sins.

Wolf is a kaleidoscopic character with unlimited potential; a parent, a teacher, healer, protector, transformer, pathfinder— Opener of The Way, Shepherd of the Fold, Coyote Trickster, Jackal Dogsbody, Lupine Lorelei—Hound of Heaven and Hell.

Sharp as obsidian; gentle as a lamb.

THE SHADOW DANCE

According to folklore, it is easy to recognize the devil, because he has no shadow. Wolf is a sometime denizen of darkness and therein casts no shadow; he could easily slip into devilish ways without being aware. More often than not, power corrupts. It is the nature of this Sign to set the pattern for others, particularly offspring and dependents. He may not allow any freedom of choice—which creates rebellion. This Sign can be extremely stubborn, and can be afflicted with emotional immaturity—may be very jealous of his territory and his rights. He may experience limitations in sharing, and in trusting others.

You may become unconsciously addicted to the excitement of replaying the traumatic drama of the past, enjoying the emotions of anger, jealousy, and danger. Throw these rascals outs. Stop jousting with windmills; tune in to the here and now. It's a good day to live!

RACCOON

KVH·LI

EP

Direction: West—Thunder and lightning; autumn displays of glorious sunsets and falling leaves; passion and transformation.

Symbol: Raccoon

Color: Copper

Stone: Amber

Element: Earth

Flower: Lady's-slipper (*Gugwe' Ulasu'la*)

Herb: Peppermint

The Sky Raccoon is Algol, a Star in the constellation Perseus. This Spirit is restless and yearns for a long-lost love. Often on a summer night, they say, he comes down to search for her and carry her away to the heavens to shine beside him. Ancient stargazers named Algol the demon star or the mischievous one because it "winks"; modern astronomers have explained that it appears to fade at times because of an eclipse by a darker, companion star.

The favorite woodland wildling of The People is the Raccoon. If taken very young it is easy to tame, and makes an affectionate, lovable, cuddly pet. These clever young critters soon learn to pick pockets and to ferret out sugary treats no matter where you hide them. Always eager to swap kisses for candy. They can open jelly jars and remove corks from bottles. They can lift the latch on a gate; it's only a matter of time before they figure out how and why to turn doorknobs. They are just full of friendly mischief. Closely related to bears: good for bear hugs. All of which is an equally apt description of the person of this Sign.

Raccoon is a magnetic personality, Leader of the Dance, songs, games, drinking, excitement, entertainment; a master mime. A very sensual person, associated with the fertility of the Earth as it is quickened by the Rain and energized to fruition by the Sun. Full of humor, gaiety, and fun, with the sparkle of champagne bubbles, flowers, and toy balloons. Always right in the middle of things. Rarely on time for any activity, but nothing happens anyway until the life of the party shows up.

The mask, a distinguished mark on the animal, is a symbol of mystery and intrigue. Possibly even of superficiality and deception. Certainly a part of putting on a show. The audience always tacitly agrees to let the actors deceive them; it's all fairytale fantasy for the titillation of the spectators, who are there to be entertained, not educated. In the jargon of the theater, "If you have a message, call Western Union!"

The animal prefers to live high up in a tree, in a hollow where a branch has fallen off. Raccoons are very sociable and family-oriented in a matrilineal manner: that is, the mother and her young live together, adding new litters until there is no more room in the den. The father goes his way after mating, having no part in rearing the young. This is startingly similar to the olde-time Cherokee lineage pattern: all children belonged to the Mother's Clan; Father was not even a blood relation.

Raccoons are very vocal; the little ones mewl and gurgle somewhat like human babies. As they grow older, they learn to bark, growl, and imitate birds. Their normal communication is a soft, churring noise with modulations. The family spends most of the daylight hours basking in the sun. At dusk they all forage for food together. With their long, searching "fingers" they find frogs, clams, mussels, crayfish, and oysters. They are fastidious diners, washing the food vigorously before eating it. They also like eggs, fruits, nuts, berries—and especially honey. In other words, they eat remarkably like people.

And strangest of all, one of their favorite foods is corn, the mainstay of the Cherokees. At the time of the Green Corn Dance, when the new corn is in the "milk," the mother can be observed teaching her cubs how to bend down the cornstalk, pull off the ear, shuck it, and holding the ear in their front paws, chomp away at the juicy kernels, just like people eating roasting ears. But here their table manners aren't so good, because they waste more than they eat. A common trait of the person of this Sign—not giving any thought to tomorrow, but living gloriously for today. Which is really the best way to go, unless it is carried to extremes.

This Day Sign is not only a performer, but an artist and a craftsman as well. Sensitive fingers create imaginative designs in weaving, pottery, jewelry, clothing. Prize paintings appear under the brush of this overflowing fountain of youth. When the artistic urge is harnessed and confined to constructive channels, the results are rewarding.

Those of this Sign are the Clowns of the Theater of Life. They need lots of attention and, just as surely as water seeks its own level, they will find a way to get it. Being multifaceted, they may seek out positions of leadership. They are not followers by nature. If leadership is beyond their reach, they will claim their rightful place in the spotlight as writers, teachers, journalists, lawyers, or media commentators. There is a tendency to promote themselves at all times, and this may attract followers who perceive in aggressiveness a kind of charisma.

Amber, the stone for this Sign, is a natural; the Greeks called it *elektron,* "Bright One," for it produces electricity when gently rubbed—giving man his first inkling of this fantastic phenomenon of nature.

This Sign is not judgmental of others and not prone to gossip. The world is so full of wondrous things to discover and handle and enjoy that there is no need to contemplate the dust at one's feet. This is a Sign whose delight is in the beauty of the Earth and the treasures thereof. Who just wants everybody to be happy.

Raccoon is the masked bandit who steals hearts, not silver and gold. Like the "Moonlight Gambler" of song, here is one who will risk everything on the turn of a card. He could be rightly called the Knave of Hearts; and she is certainly the Queen of Hearts—for these cards are really delightful characters!

THE SHADOW DANCE

There is a danger of overindulgence, supersensitivity, misuse of humor and sarcasm at the expense of the feelings of others—making fun of the underdog. Withdrawal and suppression of self-expression for fear of criticism. Feelings of inadequacy. Hiding behind a mask by playing the Fool.

It may be difficult to persevere long enough to achieve mastery in any enterprise, to build a firm foundation under a castle of dreams. Much easier to slide into the world of make-believe. Feelings of insecurity make it difficult to stand up and face any challenge. When recognition is not forthcoming, egos are bruised and the Raccoon personality may become arrogant, overbearing, and domineering.

The late President Kennedy's admonition to ask what you can do for your country, not what your country can do for you, is probably applicable here. This Sign can so easily slip into the role of a Taker, and never give anything in return. To Balance the Earth, it is necessary to participate in both the "give" and the "take" of life.

RATTLESNAKE TOOTH

KANU·GA

ᎣᎦᏃ

Direction: South—Green grass, healing herbs; living with compromise; balance of Life and Death. Guardian of The Way.

Symbol: Caduceus

Color: White

Stone: Ivory

Element: Fire

Flower: Silver-bells

Herb: Sweet grass

 The Signature of Rattlesnake Tooth in the Sky is the Rainbow. It is a delicate display of the electromagnetic rays of the sun, separated into seven basic colors: violet, indigo, blue, green, yellow, orange, and red. Daylight is white, a carousel of all colors; Night is black, the absence of color. Sun and Moon, Day and Night, Physical and Spiritual come together to display the glory of The Heavens.

Raindrops project this illusion onto the horizon: Water is the vital fluid—the Great Healer of all Life.

Rattlesnake Tooth is the Natal Day Sign of the Medicine Woman or Man, the Shaman, the Priest, the Healer—and also the Sorcerer.

The Medicine Man wore a fur cap with buffalo horns sticking up at the top. He used a terrapin shell to hold the herbs; drums, rattles, gourd dippers, and grass stems as tools of the trade; beads to diagnose and to predict the future of the patient. The Osi' (Hothouse) was the Native American hospital.

The fang of a Rattlesnake, prepared with proper prayers, was used to brush or scarify a person's skin before applying herbal preparations. Not hard enough to draw blood, just enough to absorb the medicine.

The person of this Sign is a stoic individualist, slow to anger, courteous, displaying a serene countenance no matter what turbulence is boiling around below the surface. But still water runs deep. Underneath this glossy veneer lies the kernel of discontent. Conflicting drives of compromise and rebellion wage a storm back and forth between demands of society and desire to proclaim the indisputable verities of life.

Enclosed within this protective outer shell is the heart of a fragile flower. This person is usually very touchy and easily hurt; susceptible to cuts and bruises, both physical and mental. Repression of emotional stress eventually leads to various temporary illnesses, which are recurrent but not necessarily life-threatening.

The Darkening Land of the West and the psychic secrets of individual personalities hold a fascination for this Sign. A profession that entails the exploration of these dark caverns of the Cosmos would fulfill a basic need, and help to save a fertile mind from self-destruction.

There is a very practical side to this mentality, combined with a strong investigative instinct: a desire to get to the bottom of things. They are problem-solvers, good at details, prone to deliberation, making firm decisions, and giving applicable and practical commands. They make good engineers, architects, research scientists, philosophers, and mathematicians. Performing is a good career choice, for they are en rapport with the audience.

Those born of this Sign usually achieve success and popularity because they are conservative and practical, yet ready to make a pitch for any worthy cause. Ambitious and willing to work and wait to get to the top of the ladder. They are indeed competitive, but go to great lengths to avoid direct confrontation—careful not to upset the apple cart. Here is a demonstration of a basic Cherokee philosophy: "We gonna have peace and quiet, even if we have to knock a few heads together to get it!"

The olde-time Cherokee Priestess or Priest was a direct line of communication between The People and The Great Spirit. Sacred Smoke was blown to the seven directions to create a protective shield against evil spirits. And Smoke from the open fire carried messages straight up to Heaven. The rattles, oil, and flesh of the Rattlesnake were occult ceremonial objects. Priests used them as resonant fundaments to interpret Oracles—communion with Ancestors, Spirits, and Otherworldlies.

Silver bells is an appropriate flower: the Cherokee word for the physical Rattlesnake is *Utsa'nati* "He has a bell" (referring to the rattles at the end of its tail).

The herb, sweet grass, has been used throughout the temperate zones as a medicinal from time immemorial. It is the American bulrush, which provides a haven for the mythical Infant Hero whose very life is endangered: like the biblical Moses and the Egyptian Horus, who were floated in reed baskets through the rushes to eternal life in the legends.

Dis-ease is a state of being out of balance; Healing is the bringing back into balance of the Human Spirit with The Great Spirit. This Sign is a receptacle to receive the vibrations of the Universe, a chalice to contain the holy healing waters, the Guardian of The Way—of Life and Death and Rebirth.

The supersensitivity of persons of this Sign, which can lead to intermittent ailments, is the self-same sensitivity that makes them appear to be prescient. Careful observation reveals that this so-called psychic sense is due more to paying close attention and having concern for the feelings of others than to any supernatural agent. True paranormal activity is governed by laws of physics that have not yet been discovered by man.

A person of this Sign is inclined to "keep his eyes and ears open and his big mouth shut." A Keeper of the Keys of the secret Kingdom.

Rattlesnake Tooth is the Sign of one who reaches out for the pot of gold at the end of the rainbow, who seeks buried treasure in the mountain fastness, who probes the shadows of the mystic valley. A modern-day knight errant in search of the Holy Grail, a Queen Boadicea defending the homeland. Who, all along the way, is looking for The White Path of happiness.

THE SHADOW DANCE

History reveals that outstanding visionaries of the past were declared by their contemporaries to be disturbed, crazy, evil, or at best simpleminded. There is a tendency to dump all persons who are "different" into the category of "Wicked Witch." Socrates was served hemlock, Joan of Arc burned at the stake—by her own people, those she sought to save. It is important to maintain a balance in all areas of life: neither saint nor sinner be!

Holding emotional stress inside can be very destructive. It is necessary to have a safety valve for strong feelings, or they will explode. Talking with friends is a good idea. Physical activities—walking, jogging, team sports—are good to ease internal pressure. The magician who channels his sleight-of-hand artistry into entertainment for an audience has found a healthy outlet—so long as he does not fool himself into thinking his act is for real.

REED

I'HYA

T Ꭿ ꮼ

Direction: East—Creation and Re-Creation; The Coming of Light; new directions; breaking the ties that bind.

Symbol: Reed raft and cornstalk

Color: Yellow

Stone: Jade

Element: Water

Flower: Squash blossom

Herb: Corn silk

 Reed is the Earth-reflection of the Star Chaga'see; along with Chawa'see (Flint), Reed made up the Magician Twins who led a journey to the Darkening Land of the West to bring back the Daughter of the Sun. Seven men went along to carry the casket in which to bring her back and restore her to life. This Wooden Box constellation is now known as Gemini (Gunesun'ee), and Chaga'see is called Pollux (of Castor and Pollux). In Cherokee mythology, reed (Cane, Cain) the agriculturist is the Creator Twin, and flint (Knife, Stone, Abel), who slays animals, is the Destroyer Twin.

Persons of this Sign are intellectually keen; they can bring all the elements of the Earth to bear when fighting for causes that are important to the benefit of society as a whole. They are dedicated to raising their own consciousness as well as the consciousness of all.

Reed Signs are tall or of sturdy build, statuesque, followers of the straight and narrow (as they see it). One who fights for principles; a crusader; who looks the facts of life squarely in the face, meditates, and comes up with a plan for dealing with the indisputable verities. Not one to shirk responsibilities; labors diligently when at work, but can just as wholeheartedly enjoy life when at play.

This Sign is well respected by associates, both business and social. A trailblazer, an inspiring teacher, a leader with many followers, a student of human nature; master of ancient wisdom and follower of the solemn rituals of ancestors.

This Sign has a strong mental force that probes into the interior and ferrets out the facts. Can find on the face of another person the indelibly stamped lines of character; can look into the eyes and see the mirror of the Soul. Calls a spade a spade, whether or not it is used for digging. They believe that truth is a fetish that will set you free.

And if this person will be still and listen to the breath of the Wind, she will be tuned in to the Universal Consciousness. Therein lies the font of all knowledge—of all time and all place.

The reed plant was used to make blowguns and arrow shafts. It is the Sign of a warrior who fights for the protection of all, or for causes that are just. Such people have always been held in high esteem by other members of society. It is war of conquest that steps over the line and becomes an abomination. This Sign advocates beating swords into plowshares, not only with words but with action, setting an example for others to follow.

East is the psychological direction of success and happiness, no matter what the geographic route. In the metaphor of Cherokee myth-ology, journeys are always either to or from the East, depending on whether they are toward success or defeat. The infamous Trail of Tears of the nineteenth century will go down in folklore as a forced march "from the East."

This Sign is closely associated with growth and development and change—both in *Selu* (Corn—*Zea mays*) and in humans. People were created by mixing the incarnation of the golden rays of the Sun (Corn) with the saliva of the Moon (Water). Saliva, not blood, was considered by the Cherokees to be the vital fluid of the human body.

And the cornstalk is, of course, a form of cane. Selu was the mainstay of The People, the nourishment that Mother Earth provided for Her children. A strange thing about the corn plant is that it will not reseed itself and continue to grow from one season to the next without the intervention of the hand of Man.

Along with a high regard for knowledge, persons of this Sign have an all-encompassing love affair with the great outdoors. They are tuned to the universal harmony of Nature and speak a various language. They lie down and listen to blades of grass growing; they hug trees; they converse with chipmunks; ravens call to them; deer come and eat from their hands. The only way they would ever shoot an animal is with a camera. A squirrel is for company, not for a fur coat.

Persons born under this Sign are ambitious to a fault at whatever they set their hearts on, and tend to be very conscious of their own status on the professional and social scene. They make good forest rangers, politicians, social workers, and counselors—for they communicate well and understand others.

The reed or cane plant is an excellent fire-starter. Reed types likewise build fires under things. They have miles to go and covenants to keep, and they can't wait all day to get started, and to get others involved.

In times of trial, trouble, and tribulation, it is Reed who picks up the pieces and gets things going again. There is a (Jack and the Beanstalk–type) legend about how The People once hid deep underground to escape destruction by Fire. Their return to reality was accomplished by first planting a seed. It sprouted and grew, and they all climbed up inside this hollow Reed to a bright New World.

When the World was destroyed by Flood, it was Reed rafts that floated survivors over the waters, depositing them safely on dry land. From there the Clans island-hopped over the remaining puddles and finally ended up on Turtle Island (North America).

It is predicted that the next World destruction will be by Earthquake. If and when this happens, again The People will look to Reed to beat a path through the holocaust to safety.

Reed is the Day Sign of the modern-day Moses—who leads The People away from darkness and evil into the Light of Truth: the promised land.

THE SHADOW DANCE

Before driving hard and fast to the finish line, be sure you're running toward the right goalpost. There is also danger in becoming too rigid, of falling in love with the sound of your own voice instead of taking a broad, commonsense point of view. There is the hazard of becoming self-righteous, overconfident, and egotistical.

At the same time, self-confidence and courage are essential to a person who moves into the unknown and leads others on uncharted pathways. Reed People are high achievers who have an obsession with success, but when the fire burns too hot, it leads to burnout. Usually there are built-in checks and balances, and when these fail, it's a good idea to have at least one ear open to the advice of associates.

The answer is balance. Keep in mind that "too little, too late" and "too much, too soon" are equally destructive. Sit on the fence awhile every now and then to look both ways—but don't get hung up there.

PANTHER

SAHO·NI

ᎤᎦᏂ

Direction: North—Contact with the subconscious; the hot line from nadir (interior of the Earth) to zenith (North Star).

Symbol: Panther; magician

Color: Coral

Stone: Rose quartz

Element: Air

Flower: Morning glory (sweet potato)

Herb: Blackberry

In the Sky it is the Fire Panther (*Atsila Tluntu'tsi*): Comets, Meteors, Meteorites, Shooting Stars, and Fireballs. Comets are ill omens, and Shooting Stars are lucky signs—they are Magicians and Prognosticators. Tons of meteoric dust fall on the Earth each day, and some end up as chunks of meteoric iron. The early-morning Leo constellation Meteors appearing around the middle of November are Heralds of the Coming of Light—the Cherokee New Year.

Shadow of the Sphinx—Herald of the Dawn! Panther people are creatures of the night, minions of the Sun who patrol the Dark Side from sunset to sunrise, when the Sun is traveling through the Underworld.

Panther is also called Mountain Lion, Painter, Catamount, Puma, and Cougar.

There were two Cherokee Warrior Societies: the Eagles, who were the actual soldiers, and the Panthers, who were the warriors of the dark and the night: scouts, advance guards, spies, or intelligence corps. Neither of these were men's societies, for women were admitted when they fulfilled the initiation rites. And men were allowed to join the so-called women's societies (agriculture, cooking, baby care) if they wanted to with no loss of face. In the Panther Society a female could be a regular Mata Hari; a male was a potential James Bond.

In line with the reputed belief of Native Americans that they descend from Eagles, the Cherokee myth is that The People are descended from *Saho'ni*, The Panther Spirit. Saho'ni is to the Panther as Thunderbird is to the Eagle.

This is the Day Sign of a Medicine Woman or Man, a Wizard, a Magician, a Conjurer, an Oracle. One who sees through a glass darkly the beam of light from the Spirit World, as through a somewhat transparent window. One who can gaze into a mirror, the portal to the Otherworld, and distinguish true reality from the "soul force."

This personality is aware of currents that are in the interior—unseen forces that are nevertheless quite powerful, such as earthquakes. One who needs a quiet time to channel messages from dreams and spirits, a retreat from the hurly-burly of the world for uninterrupted meditation.

This Sign is proud, conceited, haughty (overmodesty is never one of their faults), daring, presumptuous, and courageous—open-hearted, independent, dauntless, and grave. More prone to action than to talking about it. Eager for success, and willing to work for it. A stout heart ready to fight for right; a champion of the underdog, with a smile and an optimistic outlook. A dreamer who wastes no time making those dreams a reality. An intense worker, who knows when to let go and relax both body and mind.

This is a person who hides behind a mask; emotions and feelings are hidden well beneath the surface. Traumatic past experiences may cause this person to retreat to an inward sanctuary, or to build an armor against the insensitivity of the crowd. One who struggles with self-control; aggressive in the more subtle ways, may win his own way in the long stretch by avoiding direct confrontation. Often travels along secret, labyrinthine ways toward a desired goal with no outward signs of directional activity.

One seeking complete compatibility between mind, heart, and soul; seeking out partners who fit into the pattern—using the creative mind, following complex charted courses, remaining fearless in the face of constant change.

One who can look at the faults and hear the confessions of others without condemning. Whose standards for self are not necessarily the same as those for the man in the street. Who understands the frailties of the fallen without claiming equal rights to self-indulgence.

Like the animal, he is solitary, nocturnal, stealthy, secretive, and powerful. Carnivorous—or at best omnivorous—not inclined to be a vegetarian.

This may be the Sign of a competent therapist, counselor, or teacher. Spiritual, but not necessarily attached to an organized religion. Panthers may be healers, particularly healers of the body through the orientation of the mind.

Panther types have perceptive investigative powers. They see beyond the visible evidence, through the shadowy aspects to the very heart of the matter, always with sensitivity and often with psychic undertones. Shapeshifters—manipulators of manifestations.

Panther people are assertive and argumentative. They will fight to the bitter end to win a point, although they hide behind the mask of a smile—a passive-aggressive approach that may not be immediately obvious. They can be cutting and sarcastic, while at the same time subtle and devious. Satire is their forte.

These individuals have basic intelligence that can be greatly enhanced by a liberal education: psychology and the social sciences are good exploratory fields. They are outstanding in the art of communication, are often very charismatic speakers and very persuasive writers. Have an unlimited imagination, are able to visualize a whole gamut of activities, from the sublime to the ridiculous—and just might bring them all to virtual reality. They are able to brainstorm a kaleidoscope of innovations that may be as lost in the past as a dinosaur, or as extended into the future as a vacation trip to Mars. No matter that these things are quite impossible—a Panther can capture the imagination of the listener and hold him spellbound. This Sign is a builder of castles in the air—who might even put foundations under some of them.

Panther is the Sun Runner, the All-Seeing Eye, the Torchbearer who heralds the passing away of darkness and the coming of light.

THE SHADOW DANCE

Men of this Sign are in danger of becoming chauvinists and women, intellectual snobs. Some are so in love with the sound of their own voice they engage in monologues instead of conversations. They row against the current instead of learning to go with the flow.

The Great Spirit runs the Universe; never forget that. It's like working with electricity: as long as you remember the rules you can perform miracles; when you start thinking you're the boss—you get burned to a crisp.

You are a channel through which The Universal Consciousness communicates. Do not editorialize. It's Truth that's important, not anyone's personal opinion. You are the messenger, not the message. You are a modern-day Moses, who guides The People on the long journey toward the light at the end of the tunnel. It is written in the Stars: You will not reach The Promised Land.

EAGLE

UWO·HATLI

ᎣᏍᏛ Ꮨ Ꮆ

Direction: West—End of the rainbow; wings on the wind; flyway to the Stars; Aerie on Thunderstone Mountain.

Symbol: Thunderbird

Color: Silver

Stone: "Jewels of the Moon"—tektites

Element: Earth

Flower: Iris (blue flag)

Herb: Ginseng

 In the Sky Eagle is Mars, the red planet, Spirit Warrior of the Heavenly Host. His Comrades in Arms are Comets. His Thunder echoes from the Mountains and the Earth trembles at his voice; he throws Thunderbolts of Fire. He controls the airways: wind, storm, cloud, rain, hail, sleet, and snow. He is a Minion of Grandfather Moon.

According to legend, Venus appeared first as the Morning Star to tell the world that the Sun was coming. Mars was mad because he, too, wanted to be the Morning Star, and so he and Venus kept bumping together around the Earth until the Sun sorted them out on opposite sides of planet Earth. Mars threw stones, which ended up on Earth as tektites. These are greatly prized as mystic charms from outer space.

Cherokees are "Friends of Thunder"—the voice of the Thunderbird, the mighty Eagle, who patrols the skies. He is the Winged Arrow of the Moon, the Lookout on the Mountain; the diligent provider and the fierce, bold protector of the nest—keen of eye and beak and claw.

Eagles were the warrior society, the braves, the fighters, the protectors of The Nation. This was not a men's society; women were included. Likewise, men who preferred the women's society were permitted to belong with no loss of dignity. There was no sharp male-female discrimination in the old days. This is reflected in the Cherokee language: third-person singular is divided into animate, human and animate, not human—instead of he and she.

Not to suggest that The People had no interest in sex; only that they saw no need to make a "laborious elucidation of the obvious."

Persons of the Eagle Sign are ambitious, eager for high positions and coveted honors; independent; courageous and daring; high-tech, scientific, specialized; willing to put up any amount of hard work and wheeling-dealing against anticipated rewards. They are high fliers with their heads in the clouds. Status seekers. Conceited. Ready to fight their way to the top of the heap in any way that is necessary, to overcome whatever obstacles stand in the way.

This is a Sign of high hopes and anticipations, dreams and visions, cosmic consciousness and commitment—the one-way ticket to the Stars.

On a down-to-earth level, it is also the Sign of head of the household, business manager, provider par excellence, with the final decision on all questions, great and small.

This is a predominately masculine Sign. A woman of this Natal Day is inclined to leadership character; her husband may stay in and tend the children, doing the housework while she holds down an executive position. Or she may end up a *femme sole*, or in a single-parent situation. Freedom is a prized possession, no matter how it is attained.

Eagle entails husbandry, the caretaking of others: dependents, family, or associates. He deals in real estate, financial security, and inheritance. This person is most likely to be the one that other members of the extended family always come to for advice: financial and otherwise. He is the obvious choice to serve as executor of an estate; he mediates family disputes, hopefully with the wisdom of Solomon. For this is a powerful mind with the ability to weigh both sides of any question and untangle the web of controversy.

The person of this Sign is friendly and usually popular with others, despite his preference for offbeat relationships. He is a fancy-free spirit who would take off for parts unknown if it weren't for all his business deals and monkey business with countless associates, too intricate to allow instant solutions.

This Sign needs personal space, and will often distance himself from the madding crowd by retiring to the inaccessible cliffs—where he becomes the Old Man of the Mountain, consorting with the Mysterious One among the resounding echoes of the loftiest peaks. On his return, he parcels out commandments freely, turning a deaf ear to outspoken criticism.

Eagle types make their own rules as they go along; they have an unusual point of view; ahead of their own time in pioneering new developments in practical areas. Either they are psychic and have a well-developed Third Eye, or they concentrate attention on successful ventures and explain away a failure as a normal obstacle on the forward march. Otherwise, this is a critical mind, a perfectionist; open to new ideas, but only on his own terms.

This Sign is somewhat secretive; one who talks convincingly and volubly but tells you only what he wants you to know. As the Mighty Eagle uses his wings for mantling, to hide what he doesn't want to share, so this person covers up. Which only adds to the mystery, the orphic oracle quality, of his charisma that lends credence to what he does say.

The Spirit of Love and the Spirit of Victory are visualized as having wings. It appears there is a magnetism between Love and War; on the theory that opposites attract, this is understandable. Eagle is indeed the Winged Victory, also Winged Warrior—and surely the personification of Winged Moonlight, the censer of romantic love.

The Ace and Jack of Clubs are the cards suggestive of this Sign—a war club is the scepter of Mars.

An omen is a sign from the Moon; Eagle is a Moon bird; Mars is a sometime Morning Star, the Herald of the coming of the Sun.

Eagle is the sign of a bright new tomorrow!

THE SHADOW DANCE

All this power and energy should be directed to constructive, not destructive, outlets. This Sign can be intellectually stubborn—or sometimes just plain lazy. Jealousy and greed are dangers. You may easily become confused with hearing echoes, and fall in love with the sound of your own voice—or become enamored of your own image. There is a balance in caring for others; no one can be all-powerful or be all things to all people. "No man can save another man's soul." The bottom line is that each individual must save himself. Hope and encouragement are the greatest gifts.

As high as you fly, so deep is the abyss that yawns before you. "The *Eagle* has landed!" reported the astronauts. Eagle is an Earth Sign that needs to be grounded. What soars off into the wild blue yonder must, when the last flag is furled, come in for a Landing.

OWL

U·GUKU·

ᎤᎫᎫ

Direction: South—A veritable social butterfly, warm, extroverted and gregarious; sexually mature.

Symbol: Owl

Color: Snowy white

Stone: Jasper

Element: Fire

Flower: Evening primrose

Herb: Juniper berries

 In the Sky, Owl is Arcturus, the brightest Star in the constellation Boötes. The Cherokee Bear constellation (Ursa Major) includes the Big Dipper plus four Stars in Boötes. The bowl is the Bear, followed by Seven Hunters: Robin, Chickadee, and Buzzard are the stars in the handle; Pigeon, Blue Jay, Owl (Arcturus), and Sparrow are in Boötes. As above, so below—Owl is a hunter, who stands for the wisdom and ability of all great hunters: the cunning of a fox, the tenacity of a bulldog, and the strength of a bear.

Owl (also Uku or Oukah) is the title of the White or Peace Chief, usually a Medicine Woman or Man. This person has the responsibility of interpreting the visions and nightmares sent by Black Obsidian Butterfly, spirit of the dark maze of the human subconscious.

Owl Signs are people of long life, and are likely to amass wealth somewhere along the way. They enjoy good health and a good physique—muscular, tall, hale and hearty, vigorous and robust—free from disease.

Owl Signs are very talented and have an excellent store of knowledge. They are deep thinkers, hardened to life, realistic, practical, every inch the "Wise Old Owl." They have much to offer the world. But they are strong-willed, have rigid convictions, and are not easily swayed by the arguments of others. Owl is inclined to be bold and authoritative—a person who must take control of situations, using force if necessary.

Of a serious nature, persons of the Owl Sign are grave, calm, discreet, eloquent—often gathering disciples around them; they may be teachers, fond of giving advice as well as setting a good example. They shine in the area of dispensing advice to others. They have usually come up the hard way; faced many challenges; paid close attention to solutions to problems; already know what works and what doesn't. This qualifies them to pass along the advantages of their own experience. They are able to analyze a situation and come up with a solution.

Owl Signs have good, down-to-earth business sense. They aspire to the role of boss. They make good managers, have what amounts to a compulsion to climb the corporate ladder to CEO; as top dog, they like to control the big picture, with under-managers to carry out instructions from the top.

Owl types are very status-conscious; they are concerned with their own position in the social order. They seek authority and position, are acutely aware of their own importance at all times. This often leads to self-consciousness around those in a position to judge them.

They have high standards, not only for their own actions but for those around them, often feeling it a duty to censure evil wherever they find it. The Owl's head is capable of turning all the way around; this means they have eyes in the back, and don't miss much. And they are recognizably insensitive to the frailties of their fellow men.

Because they themselves fought tooth and talon for their place in the sun, they feel that others should do the same.

They have a deep fear of rejection, which can leave them at the mercy of overaggressive, domineering personalities. Females who have been subjected to father domination tend to become entangled in relationships with father figures. Strangely enough, although there is much conflict with authority figures, Owl signs feel strongly impelled to take over authority for themselves. And although they struggle mightily to remain high man on the totem pole, not a few end up being victims. Many female Owl types become so browbeaten and insecure that they choose a husband who maintains the rigid structure of domination of the Owl personality, and the female becomes the victim within it.

Owl types are the personification of the struggle between superiority and inferiority. They are a mixture of differences, discrepancies, and imbalance. To control these conflicts, they insist on rules—laws that apply to everyone, regardless of status. "Let the punishment fit the crime!" They are strong on teaching The People that dereliction of duty, idleness, lying, theft, drunkenness—breaking any law—brings on certain punishment. This applies to the laws of both Heaven and Earth.

Mixed in with this serious, fatalistic, arcane personality is a bright streak of comic relief. This Sign has a great sense of humor that may come out at the most unexpected times. Although it is mostly sarcastic and cynical, it is sharp and keen and to the point.

"It's lonely at the top"—These persons indeed must have much time alone, separate, solitary. They retire to their own private mountaintop to meditate in order to establish wise counsel within themselves. This is difficult for the average person to understand.

Owl is the Mystic Ferryman who guides Earthlings on the return path to the Stars. The length of the spinal column in your own body is the Ferryman's Staff, which points from the Earth plane to the Sky Vault. Through meditation you are able to tune in to the Universal Consciousness, in the perfect unfolding of the pattern and the meaning of the Cosmos.

One of unpredictable fates and unusual occurrences, Owl is a part of the wildness of the Earth and the everlasting enigma of creation.

Owl holds aloft a torch of White Light that keeps the unfathomable Darkness at bay.

THE SHADOW DANCE

Owl types may be insensitive in their personal relationships. They have little patience with the shortcomings of the common herd. Since they themselves have worked very hard to overcome obstacles, they feel that others should do the same.

The worst thing that can happen to those of this Sign is to lose face. Fortunately, this rarely happens.

Sometimes the roar of the crowd is so loud in your ears, you fail to hear the whispering of a butterfly's wings. The White Light is within you; if you do not find it there, you will find it nowhere.

Don't let tyrants bully you; listen to your inner voice. Insecurity can make you a victim of your own design.

A gentle reminder: The Great Spirit runs the Universe—it is neither your privilege nor your responsibility to do so.

HERON

GUWI·SGUWI

JꙨꙨJꙨ

Direction: East—Return of Light and New Life; reawakening from the journey to the Otherworld. The Cosmic Egg drops.

Symbol: Heron, Cosmic Egg

Color: Green

Stone: Mother-of-pearl

Element: Water

Flower: Bird-of-paradise

Herb: Honey locust

 In the Sky, the Northern Cross is the Tree of Life, beside the Milky Way River; and perched atop it is Guwi'sguwi, the Cherokee Heron Spirit Bird, comparable to the Egyptian Phoenix. The Star is now called Deneb. Myth has it that in a time of chaos, a beautiful young Maiden (Heron) fell from the Sky Tree, down, down, down into the Primordial Sea. Turtle came to the surface of the water and rescued her. She nested there on Turtle's back, and laid her Cosmic Egg.

Every five thousand years or so, the Sun is captured by the Lord of Darkness, Evening Star, but Heron Spirit triumphs with the Resurrection and the Light.

Heron is the Sign of movement, of perpetual motion, of Life Everlasting from birth to rebirth. It is the action of recycling, of salvaging all things of value from one world to another, from seedtime to harvest and back again. It is generations of regeneration. It is the realization that time and tide wait for no one; they go on forever.

Persons of this Day Sign have these characteristics of looking to the future to save the planet for all of us, for our children, and for our children's children. This includes the environmentalists and those who protest cruelty to animals. Those of this Sign are very likely to be found taking in stray animals or nursing a wounded bird. They fight for the rights of the underdog at all levels; it is a labor of love, for not a sparrow falleth . . . . and not even one tiny mustard seed should be wasted, lest The People go hungry on the morrow. There is never any doubt that tomorrow will come; it always has—always will.

This is the Sign of a mentally alert, rational, progressive but down-to-earth individual; open-minded and future-oriented, yet hidebound and opinionated; surrounded by controversy.

These persons have a generally optimistic outlook; they laugh easily; have a great sense of humor. They enjoy the camaraderie of give and take without a chip on the shoulder. If they lose a round, they just set a stubborn jaw and refuse to play anymore. In fact, they may never bother to talk to you again. They're not the sort who telephones to tell you how cool they've grown. They rarely threaten. However, since they usually end up rich, prosperous, and powerful, they are more likely to cancel your Christmas bonus.

Persons of this Sign hold the magic of ministry, medicine, marketing, and matchmaking, which embraces both the masculine mantra of oom and the feminine mantra of maa.

Heron Signs have a great faith in the potential of the human soul; they believe that the world proceeds according to divine plan, and that sensible and logical solutions can be found for every problem. Their strength comes from the power of their own convictions. They do well as pastor of a church or a minister of religious education, particularly working with youth—coaching the ball team, for instance.

The momentum of motion in this Sign includes the rocking motion which, like cradle rocking, soothes and relaxes and lulls anyone to sleep. This person has healing hands and, even when she's not touching a living entity (animal, vegetable, or mineral), can create peace of mind, mental and physical balance—which is the essence of wellness. Healing crystals literally come alive under their hands. They talk to plants; herbs will work for them. A career in alternative medicine could be quite successful for Heron types.

The person of this Sign could also be a super sales representative—even selling iceboxes to Eskimos or neckties to South Sea Islanders; or ideas to the masses on a grand scale, like politicians. Unshakable belief in one's product makes a good sales pitch.

To act as a negotiator is a natural for this Sign. The ability to see a situation from all sides makes it possible for Heron to point up a profit for all participants. To see a need in one place and fill it with a service from another is the kind of cooperative effort that keeps the world going around smoothly: to match supply and demand. The job of matchmaker for marriages has gone out of style, or at least that's what they say, but many still make a hobby of it. On the other hand, management of charitable organizations is a wide-open field.

This Sign often shows outstanding ability as an artist, particularly in the field of music. Heron loves and enjoys all of the arts, either as a performer or simply as one who appreciates the finer things of life. Here is a very satisfactory field to follow, for this Sign is very independent and resents supervision of any kind. Anything that can be done solo is definitely preferred, even if it means irregular hours and very little job security. If leadership positions are not forthcoming, they will work longer hours for less pay rather than submit to rigid conformity. A caretaker in a wildlife preserve, for example—they may have trouble staying with the same position over a long period of time unless the job itself offers a wide variety of loosely supervised activity.

This is the Sign of a dreamer, one who has a fertile imagination, who can transform a vision into a reality, can take cobwebs and weave them into a gossamer veil; who can wander the maze and find the Heart of Earth; who has one foot in a deep dark cave, and the other on a fleecy white cloud—who can gather the gifts of Gaia and put them to practical use.

Heron is a bright Star in the Sky for all mortals; the Herald of a Golden Age.

THE SHADOW DANCE

It is important to strike a balance between conflict and compliance. There is a thin line separating genius and foolhardiness, and it is necessary to walk the tightrope over the two.

Holding a grudge is negative; narcissism is limiting; insecurity resulting in timidity is demoralizing; eccentricity can become too far out; and a troublemaker without just cause is nothing but a nuisance.

When your plans and processes are way out ahead of your time, don't be impatient with others who are stuck in the horse-and-buggy mode. Don't try to save the whole world before the sun is south.

And don't forget to stand up for your own rights, as well as the rights of others. The importance of the individual and the group must be given separate but equal consideration.

There is too much to do and too little time; a few rounds of rest and relaxation will erase the wrinkles of recurring controversy.

FLINT

DAWI·SGALA

Ꮅ Ꮎ Ꮝ Ꮿ Ꮤ

Direction: North—Stellar ray of crystal-clear Truth; bridge to the Moon; the last way station before entering The Way.

Symbol: Flint knife

Color: Steel blue

Stone: Diamond

Element: Air

Flower: Indian paintbrush

Herb: Holly

 Flint in the sky is Chawa'see, or Castor of the Castor and Pollux Twins in the constellation Gemini. Chaga'see (Reed) and Chawa'see are the so-called Hero Twins, the Magicians of Cherokee myth. In time of trouble, The People often called on them for help. Castor, who appears first in the evening in the west, personifies darkness, which is the time of clearing the decks for action, the gathering of manna, and the renewal of thrust to meet the challenges that are to come—as sure as day follows night.

Pollux then appears first at dawn in the east, bringing forth light: the end of night.

Long, long ago, according to myth, Flint Spirit was beamed down to *Du'stayalun'yi* (Thunder Rock), where he shone like the Sun and spoke in the voice of Thunder. He gave The People the Sacred Venus Calendar, fixed the days of festivals, feast, and fasting, and promised to watch over Earthlings for all Time.

And the Flint person endeavors to keep that covenant. He is a creator, an originator, an innovator. Opener of The Way to new pathways. He has a keen mind and a lively curiosity to explore beyond the confines of the status quo. He is well read, researching fundamental knowledge for the joy of learning. He has enthusiasm for new subjects; he initiates new patterns of invention. He inspires mental expansion in others, and stretches the mind to the outside limits of any capability in physical and spiritual development. He changes the static to the dynamic.

Flint knows and knows that he knows. He thoroughly enjoys sharing information on highly technical subjects; is a good conversationalist, open to new ideas, intuitive and analytical information that leads to new directions; a leader who sees the way ahead clearly and is willing to move boldly forward, taking others with him. Discipline is his forte; he brings about change; often separation and destruction are necessary to make room for the new structures.

The stellar ray of Truth that Flint beams toward Earth is a

crystal sword cast down along the path of a lightning flash. The blade lunges straight through to impale its target, bringing about a transformation; when this is accomplished, it shatters and scatters to the four corners.

Flint is lighting incarnate, solidified and materialized. A lightning-struck tree has special healing powers. And the use of sacred stones that have living power in them, as well as other sacred things, to give force to ritual and divination, is a practice that goes back to the dawn of history and beyond.

The Cherokee word for Flint also means "smooth," "glass," "ice," "hail." The Jack of Diamonds and Queen of Diamonds are the cards that personify the outward appearance of the Sign. But there is fire beneath that calm surface; like a volcano, it may erupt at any time. This is the Firestone that strikes fire, the tool that shapes raw material into something useful—and sometimes beautiful. Somewhere in that maze of mirrors, obscured by a smoke-screen, lies the naked truth; it is this Sign who cuts away the dross, who strips away all illusion and releases the healthy growth within. Time is of the essence. Decisiveness—to seize the moment—results in much good fortune.

This Sign is the animus, or masculine aspect, of the human personality, which is as elusive as a will-o'-the-wisp, nebulous as a cloud, unsubstantial as the smoke that carries messages up to The Great Spirit—and as powerful. Lightning is the force of electricity, which is the greatest power known to man, and is also the most metaphysical. As hard to hold as quicksilver, yet as bright and shining as a silver dollar. Which indicates a paradox of personality traits in Flint that lead to magnificent destiny if reined and tamed—and to chaos and destruction given a lack of direction.

Such is the dynamics of masculine energy: the power to move a mountain when dedicated to constructive endeavor, and the horror of a holocaust when allowed to run amok.

In earliest times Flint represented the knife with which the hunter killed game; in other times it was the sheepherder, who killed for food and sacrifice; at the present time it is the technologist who builds roads, bridges, buildings, big cities, factories, airplanes, and war machines—beating the plowshares back into swords—tools of destruction. He is carrying the civilized world as far as possible away from the feminine characteristics of nature: agriculture, peace, and pastoral village life.

In the old Cherokee culture a woman was welcomed into any work she chose if she could pass the initiation tests. Just as any man could take up agriculture, cooking, or baby care—without any loss of face. A woman born to this Sign has technical skills that need to be put to practical use, or needs to fulfill a more active, positive, supportive position of leadership. Single-parent households and women in the work force have become commonplace in today's world.

Flint is an old Sign that came to Earth from the Stars, and will eventually go around full circle, returning to the place from whence he came. He has steered us into a computer age of virtual reality, our own high-tech Silicon Valley of which he is the master craftsman. He has carried us to the Moon, and that's the last stopping-off place on the way to eternity.

Flint is the Transformer whose raison d'être is to bring things to a head and clear away the detritus, to wipe the slate clean for the dawning of a bright new tomorrow.

THE SHADOW DANCE

This Sign is self-sacrificing but prone to martyrdom, suppressed anger, and the green-eyed monster, jealousy. Vanity is a dangerous pitfall; too much about absorption in personal appearance and performance can lead to pompous self-consciousness. Indecision about cooperation versus self-interest means failure to accomplish anything at all—a futile running-back-and-forth between goalposts.

Might does not make right. A man does not have to beat his wife or be a social dropout to prove his manhood; the finer qualities of masculinity are displayed through acceptance of responsibilities to family and community. Neither does a woman have to wear the pants in the family to proclaim her worth.

Look into the mirror and see the image of yourself; acknowledge the shadowy parts that stand between you and a Star. You have the gift of insight; tune in to the Light!

REDBIRD

TOTSU'HWA

V ꝺ Ᏽ

Direction: West—Dreamtime underneath the tree; portal to the Otherworld; honeycomb of peace and love and life eternal.

Symbol: Redbird

Color: Royal purple

Stone: Amethyst

Element: Earth

Flower: Apple blossom

Herb: Wild strawberry

 Redbird is the Earth-reflection of Alcyone, the youngest and brightest of the Pleiades Star Cluster in the constellation Taurus. Sometime in the 1800s an astronomer discovered that Alcyone is the central sun of the universe, the rightful Heart of Heaven—but academia refused to believe it.

Lightning is visible evidence of the presence of Redbird Spirit in the Sky.

According to Cherokee legend, The People came to Earth originally from the Pleiades, and it is possible to return to *Nun'dogun'yi*, The Sun Land. Other Peoples of the world share these same legends.

Redbird is the Daughter of the Sun Spirit and is therefore the Sign of Fire, Sun's alter ego on Earth. Like red-hot lava that erupts and spews forth over the land, this Sign bubbles over with volatile emotions.

This is a feminine Sign, the hand that rocks the cradle. There is a loving rapport with youngsters; they sit at her feet and listen to stories of all the wonders of this world and the next. She reflects the gentleness and wide-eyed innocence of the mind of a child.

The Daughter of the Sun is a symbol of nurturing, the Princess Royale who takes over the care of the old, frail, downtrodden, forgotten—the lame, the sick, and the halt—and finds for them a place in the sun.

The masculine side of this Sign is the poet, the gentle romantic who jousts with windmills in pursuit of truth and beauty; the lad who loves not wisely, but too well.

Cherokees are "Friends of Thunder." The Two Little Red Men of Thunder (the Thunder Boys) are sons of Red Man, the Moon. They are the vocal half of Thunder and Lightning—companions of Rain and Cloud and Hurricane.

Lightning marks the path of the Redbird's flight. It is the visible hot line between Earth and Sky, blending solar and planetary atmospheric energy with the energy of Earth. Flashes of Lightning compound vital elements with the essence of plants and animals to promote growth, thus ensuring the seasonal return of fertility. It triggers the union of Sun and Moon, of Earth and Heaven for the perpetuation of Life, without which the Land would be barren and empty.

The person of this Sign is full of zest, curiosity, and imagination; a dreamer of dreams; a crusader, a builder of castles in the air. A natural energizer, who turns people on to ideas.

Lightning adds spiritual force to the human body by way of "lightning in the blood" that the Medicine Woman (or Man) feels within her own body, her own pulse. Direct body-to-body vibration can be even stronger than words or mind-to-mind communication. The key to extrasensory perception (ESP) and access to the wisdom of the Ancestors lies in the ability to bestir the blood to speak. Sheet lightning, rebounding to the seven directions, is the source of illumination to the path through the Underworld to the Otherworld, and the Opening of The Way.

The sacred stones used in rituals and divination—flint, obsidian, crystals, and others that have living power in them—are made by lightning when it strikes the ground.

Lightning gives to persons of this Sign an intuition and supersensitivity to the Universal Consciousness. However, it is necessary to tune in to Nature's own electric power system, and filter out the superficial static.

Fire is a rite of purification and spiritual transformation. The flame is personified as Ancient Red, and the ashes as Ancient White. Persons of this Sign are versatile, many-faceted, friendly, interesting, and consequently popular. They often talk for a living: make good teachers, for they are easily understood. They can be artists, musicians, and singers, particularly of a vintage style. They respect tradition: are more inclined to imitate than to break new ground.

They are drawn to philosophy and spirituality, and in earlier times to midwifery. Natural healing is the feminine forte: chewed basswood bark was applied to a rattlesnake bite, for instance, because of an occult connection with Thunder. This tree is believed to parry the thrust of Lightning.

Fire can burn furiously and consume everything it touches, or it can smolder in the ashes as an ember until it is again fanned into flame. Like restless youth that never grows old—it just keeps on going, and going, and going . . . .

The Queen of Spades and the Jack of Spades are the cards that relate to this Sign, which is close to the Earth. Spades are the diggers who prepare the soil, uproot the weeds, and tend the beds to full fruition.

Redbird is the fertility Sign, the Caldron of Creation, the germ of regeneration, the planter of seeds:

> Tuck them in with soft brown earth
>   until they're snug and warm;
> little bulbs must never feel,
> tender bulbs must never feel
>   the Winter's cold and storm.
> Now we'll leave the baby plants
>   and let them go to sleep;
> till the Springtime bids them wake
> when the Springtime bids them wake
>   through frost and snow they'll peep.

The Redbird throws the switch that turns on the lights all over the world, and engages the gears that grind out the sands of time.

THE SHADOW DANCE

Fire is a miracle worker to the benefit of mankind when it is controlled; when it runs riot it causes mass destruction. Such is the fire of this Sign. There is need for balance. Emotions are inclined to flare up, or to seethe internally. And there is a middle ground between neatness and sterility. You have a love for all humanity, all nations and races; it's the one-on-one encounters that you find hard to handle.

> You are pioneering New Frontiers;
> You are experiencing Transformation;
> You are probing the Crucible of Change.

Separate trash from your treasures; gather up your doubts, fears, insecurities—and cast them into the Fire. Burn your bridges to all past failures and face front to the future. Don't play your tragedies over and over in your mind like a broken phonograph record.

Use Fire to forge the tools of your trade.

FLOWER

GUN'TSI

EK

Direction: South—Midsummer: Earth is in full bloom; energy of love and creativity; temporary beauty of flowers.

Symbol: Sunflower disk (Eye of the Sun)

Color: Gold

Stone: Ruby

Element: Fire

Flower: Sunflower

Herb: Red cedar

 The Sky Sign here is the Sun, Place of Abode of The Great Spirit, *Agehyagugun,* whose cyclic movement represents the cyclic pattern of all Life. Fire is "Sun on Earth"—or Ancient White, Her alter ego. Sunshine is the energy that combines with the fertility of the Moon to renew the Earth. Their children include Redbird, Morning Star, and the Two Little Red Men of Thunder.

The Sun not only creates and sustains all Life, it is the super-communicator, the way station that relays messages from other Stars in the galaxy. The Redbird Star, Alcyone of the Pleiades Cluster, is a source of this extraterrestrial broadcasting. Sunspots are the key to deciphering the code.

Persons of the Flower Sign are channels for receiving these transmissions; they might like to cooperate with SETI (Search for Extra-Terrestrial Intelligence) and help in solving the cosmic communication question.

Flower is a natural channel for the rays of love radiating from the Heart of Heaven; an idealist, an artistic dreamer; devoted, romantic, demonstrative; one who is aware of the beauty of the Earth and the wonders thereof: the miracle of the transformation of sunlight to the yellow butterfly, flitting from blossom to blossom, gathering the pollen of positive thinking, and distributing it to the four winds.

The Night Sun, after setting in the west, arouses the Black Obsidian Butterfly, who is the nighthawk predator striking terror into the hearts of humans, and insinuating evil visions into the minds of the unwary.

This Sign needs to combine realism and idealism; to enjoy the light, and to cope with darkness—which Opens the Way to the best of two worlds.

Persons of this Sign speak the living language of Light, which ignites the consciousness of others. They could charm the birds right out of the trees with their soft talk, both in public and on a one-to-one basis. They are gentle as a Dove, that minion of the Sun who stands for "peace at any price." Any fight for the cause of peace would have to be sub-rosa—being careful not to disturb the placid waters.

These Flower persons are not to be confused with the so-called "Flower Children" of the sixties who wore a posy to advertise their pursuit of the impossible dream. Flower types may share the same dreams, but they differ basically in that they are willing to oil the machinery with elbow grease.

This Sign is a knight errant seeking out the honor and the glory, a believer in fame as the name of the game, blatantly drawn to the glamorous lifestyle, riding the social merry-go-round and reaching for the brass ring, gathering disciples and listening for the thunder of applause, looking for the winning lottery ticket and seeing the glitter of diamonds.

And why not? Gold is the color of courage and indicates an opportunity for wealth.

Career opportunities for those of this Sign include the arts, crafts, weaving, songwriting, jewelry and metalworking, entertainment, fund-raising. They incline to be master craftsmen; intellectuals will find satisfaction even in the exact sciences such as mathematics. Whatever the chosen direction, there is a need for a creative outlet, which can be fulfilled in a hobby—either making things or contemplating the phenomena of nature.

Women lean toward the decorative arts such as fancy breads and cakes, embroidery, beautiful clothing, personal adornment. Men are in no way excluded from these arts; Cherokee men were quick to take up glass beadwork when it was introduced in the eighteenth century.

This Sign is a good team worker, and may find satisfaction in coordinating the artistry of others. All tend to be clean-cut, hard-working, diligent, eager to put their own hands to the wheel, working away with sunny esprit de corps.

Flower is very concerned with personal relationships; works better in double harness; experiences joy in sharing. This is a mixer, not a loner; one who is comfortable with people, who could sit at a typewriter in Grand Central Station and write a poem without feeling distracted. Companionship is the key. Emotions are more satisfying when discussed with friends; trouble is a lighter load when divided in half. There is room for two in a buffalo robe—and it's much warmer when shared.

The disk wheel of the Sunflower as the Eye of the Sun is a mandala that portrays a Star as the Center of the Universe. The multiple petals represent the many rays extending out from the Great Central Sun. Although it is generally agreed that the Cherokees recognize seven directions, there are indeed an infinite number of directions around the horizon and up and down, all around the sphere. Meditation on this mandala soothes the troubled soul and tames the stress and tension of everyday living. It will help keep you calm and collected, will let you ride the waves without capsizing your canoe.

The Face of the Flower follows the Sun from sunrise through high noon to sunset each day, gathering the fire of creativity, illuminating harmony and balance, resonating peace and continuity within the human spirit.

This Sign is the Chalice of the Infinite, the Caldron of Creation, the Herald of a planetary Golden Age. Here rests the temporary beauty of the flower—both the times of sowing and reaping, and the dark time when the field is fallow.

Flower is a golden-winged bird, singing its heart out to The Golden Sun.

THE SHADOW DANCE

Flower types strive for perfection in an imperfect world. Disillusionment inevitably follows in the wake of such unrealistic expectations. But they are inclined to hang on to their ideals long after the cause is lost. Although they display ardent affection for friends and soul mates, they tend to require equal enthusiasm in return, which sooner or later leads to a breakdown in communication.

There is a lack of understanding and respect for the ideology of others. There is a tendency to hang on long after the blossom has turned to dust. The balance of give and take can be missing, and they find themselves alone, living with their own daydreams.

Come down out of the clouds and plant your feet on terra firma. Get real. Perfection is a goal we all reach for, but cannot expect to attain.

The Thirteen Numbers

There were thirteen days in a Cherokee week—that's the length of time it takes the sun to travel across the sky the same distance that the moon covers in one day. So the thirteen-day week is one moon day. The present seven-day week of the Gregorian calendar is calculated by the four phases of the moon—new moon, first quarter, full moon, and last quarter ($4 \times 7 = 28$).

Cherokees used the vigesimal system of counting (by twenties) instead of the decimal (by tens) as used by the United States today. Numbers were read from the bottom up, instead of to the right and left of a decimal point. There was little or no concern for fractions. They also read sentences from right to left and from bottom to top, identifying time periods by the last day instead of the first; they placed the zero before 1 instead of after 9, so the week was numbered from 0 through 12 instead of from 1 to 13. But following that style would really make a muddle, so we bow to current custom to avoid unnecessary confusion. It is enough to keep the number symbols reading from the bottom up—them things won't fit into your computer nohow.

A cowrie shell is the symbol of the feminine—from which all things are created. Thus it is also the glyph for 0. From nothing arises all things.

One dot is equal to 1 unit, and one bar is equal to 5 units. Their position in the figure indicates their value. The bottom (or only) line represents units, thus:

Zero	One	Four	Five	Seven

Nine	Ten	Thirteen	Fifteen	Nineteen

The line above units is twenties:

•	(1	×	20	=	20)
⬤	(0	×	1	=	0)
				=	20

•••	(3	×	20	=	60)
——	(5	×	1	=	5)
				=	65

The next line up is four hundreds (20 × 20):

•	(1	×	400	=	400)
••	(2	×	20	=	40)
•	(6	×	1	=	6)
				=	446

And so on, ad infinitum. A World (eon, era, or sun) was approximately 5,200 years.

•••‗	(13	×	400	=	5,200)
⬤	(0	×	20	=	0)
⬤	(0	×	1	=	0)
				=	5,200

This count of years in a World, like everything else in nature, was approximate. So nobody knows exactly when this present World will end—even if they knew exactly when it began—which they don't.

Previous Worlds have ended in cataclysm, such as Flood (the Christian biblical flood, for example), Fire, Ice, and Wind. The prediction is that the present World will be brought to an end by Earthquake. But as the TV funny goes: Don't quit your job yet—it may not come in our time.

Four is the most sacred number: as the four quarters of the Earth, the Four Seasons, the four phases of human life (Maiden, Mother, Mage, and Midnight).

Five marks the center of the structure of horizontal space. The Cherokees see this as the First Direction (instead of the Fifth), for it is the place that All Directions are relative to.

Seven signifies the Center-of-Being, the Four Directions, the zenith and nadir: the minimum number to completely define all the time and space that exists. The Seven Clans in its largest sense refers to all People of all Time and Place.

Forty-nine (7×7) is the Foundation-of-the-Earth Sacred Formula.

Fifty-two is the number of solar years it takes for the Civil Calendar to coincide with the 260-day Sacred (Venus) Calendar.

Each one of the following Thirteen Numbers, when added to the Day Sign, gives valuable specific information that applies to that Sign.

THE NUMBER 1 •

One is the number of the Sun, Spirit of Creation and Re-Creation. It intensifies all personality traits of the Sign. It is the pulsation ray of unity with Self and with the Universe: light of the world, rainbow of diversity; magnetic force that brings cosmic vibrations into harmony; chalice of the infinite.

Mother of invention, beginnings, awakenings, individual expression, artistic urges.

Initiator. Opener of The Way.

THE NUMBER 2 ••

Two is the number of the pulsation ray of Dual Polarity, the two opposites that also complement each other. The essence of the

Universe is to balance these Sacred Twins: Good and Evil, Night and Day, Master and Slave, Black and White, Yin and Yang— Male and Female. Spirits maintain a perfect balance, and are therefore neither male nor female.

Cherokees dance to Balance the Earth; you have an invitation to The Dance.

THE NUMBER 3 •••

Three is a triangle, universal sign of the female principle. It is the heartbeat of the Cosmos, the rippling rhythm of the river of life, the flight of the birds and the bees, the Moon-of-Deflowering—the gestes of the Lords and Ladies of the Land. It tells of creativity, crystals, charms, caprice; all in the name of growth and generation.

A nature lover, who celebrates the beauty of the Earth and the bounty thereof.

THE NUMBER 4 ••••

Four is the number of the vines at the four corners of Turtle Island that suspend it from the Sky Vault. This is the most sacred number, which embraces the cycle of the seasons, circles of the Sun, phases of the Moon: the four elements that are the foundation of all life on Earth. It represents the four-partite world of land and sea and sky and nether regions.

A basic fundamental, spiritual, grounded personality anchored to the Sacred Mountain.

THE NUMBER 5 —

Five is the number of Venus, stellar Spirit of Love and War. This is a very young and feisty feminist, somewhat recently thrust from the arms of Jupiter; she dashed about as a Comet, clashed with

Mars, and threatened planet Earth for half a millennium before settling down to the orderly life of a planet: a veritable diamond in the night sky.

Here shines a sparkling, bubbling personality—who boils over at friction overload.

THE NUMBER 6 ⚊

Six is the number of the Moon, called Sixkiller, the Great Hunter. He is also the King of Hearts, for myth has it that he is the sire of all Cherokee babies. And the Man in the Moon is a 'Coon. Raccoon, that is—the Love Bandit. He is a man of many phases; also known as *Une'hlanun'hi*, The Apportioner, for he measures out the months of the Lunar Calendar.

This is an incurable romantic, in pursuit of the true, the good, and the beautiful.

THE NUMBER 7 ⚌

Seven is the number of two sets of six steps: up one side of a pyramid and down the other, adding up to twelve; plus the landing in between—a total of thirteen. The top level is the ritual Seventh Heaven, Platform of the Sky. Seven is a sacred balance of the Dual Polarities; seven times seven is the most Holy of Holies: Foundation of the Earth Ritual.

This is a potential Keeper of the Eternal Flame of The People: a shamanistic type.

THE NUMBER 8 ⚏

Eight is the number of Earth and its harmonic resonances. It embraces the female-male duality of the fourfold nature of divinity: the four corners, seasons, elements, winds, primal rivers, and mountains. It is the act of starting over from the beginning, of repeating the octave—the frequency level at which all organic matter vibrates. And crystals, of course.

This is a partnership person who understands human relationships: like The Seven Clan Plan.

THE NUMBER 9 ••••

Nine is the number of the World Tree at the end of the Sacred Path, on the edge of the abyss. It is the portal to the magical and mystical land of the ennead wanderers of the nightland: Mercury, Venus, Mars, Jupiter, Uranus, Saturn, Neptune, Pluto, and Chiron. Part of the woof and warp of the tapestry of time and tide. Metamorphosis from caterpillar to butterfly.

An individualist who marches to a different drummer; tuned in to parapsychology.

THE NUMBER 10 ══

Ten is the number of the flow of manna between Heaven and Earth, the equal sign of the "as above, so below" concept that every Star in the Sky has a mirror image here on Earth. Two bars (══) counts ten—half of the duality of twenty, which is the base of the Cherokee vigesimal number system. In the beginning was the computer with ten fingers and ten toes . . . .

A person who guides others along the way; who can braid tangled threads into a lifeline.

THE NUMBER 11 ≛

Eleven is the number of the crossroads on the Astral Trail, that Maze of the Migration of the human Soul: from birth through the Return Journey to the Stars. The place to stop and confirm a

Guiding Star. The action of peeling off outworn husks and freeing the kernel within. From here on out it is necessary to move onward and upward like an arrow in flight.

Here is a mind like a steel trap; it knows to hold tight—and to let go; each in its own time!

THE NUMBER 12 ••

Twelve is the number of Ulunsu'ti, the Magic Crystal, the six-sided stone that is half of the dual polarity of Twelve. It amplifies electrical current—and prayers and wishes, and sensitivity; it heals by bringing the body's natural vibrations into sync; it starts a fire by concentrating the rays of the Sun, or energizing the heart and mind.

One who spiritually turns on the light, turns up the heat, and starts the motor running.

THE NUMBER 13 •••

Thirteen is the number of the Universe: all there is, was, or ever shall be. There is an umbilical cord that stretches from the North Star to the Navel of the Earth, the union of Father Sky and Mother Earth. The Quadrinity of Spirit, Nature, Fellow Man, and Self comes around full circle to The Place of The Beginning—

World without End!

eeyah'!

This is:

THE SUN PRIESTESS

THE BELOVED WOMAN

THE VOICE OF THE GREAT SPIRIT.

Ephemeris

 Use this chart to find your own Natal Day.

Date		Animal	Date		Animal
Jan. 11, 1900	I	RABBIT	Nov. 6, 1900	I	DEER
Jan. 24, 1900	I	TURTLE	Nov. 19, 1900	I	FLOWER
Feb. 6, 1900	I	PANTHER	Dec. 2, 1900	I	REED
Feb. 19, 1900	I	DEER	Dec. 15, 1900	I	TWINS
Mar. 4, 1900	I	FLOWER	Dec. 28, 1900	I	REDBIRD
Mar. 17, 1900	I	REED	Jan. 10, 1901	I	RATTLESNAKE TOOTH
Mar. 30, 1900	I	TWINS			
Apr. 12, 1900	I	REDBIRD	Jan. 23, 1901	I	SERPENT
Apr. 25, 1900	I	RATTLESNAKE TOOTH	Feb. 5, 1901	I	FLINT
			Feb. 18, 1901	I	RACCOON
May 8, 1900	I	SERPENT	Mar. 3, 1901	I	DRAGON
May 21, 1900	I	FLINT	Mar. 16, 1901	I	HERON
Jun. 3, 1900	I	RACCOON	Mar. 29, 1901	I	WOLF
Jun. 16, 1900	I	DRAGON	Apr. 11, 1901	I	HEARTH
Jun. 29, 1900	I	HERON	Apr. 24, 1901	I	OWL
Jul. 12, 1900	I	WOLF	May 7, 1901	I	THE RIVER
Jul. 25, 1900	I	HEARTH	May 20, 1901	I	WHIRLWIND
Aug. 7, 1900	I	OWL	Jun. 2, 1901	I	EAGLE
Aug. 20, 1900	I	THE RIVER	Jun. 15, 1901	I	RABBIT
Sept. 2, 1900	I	WHIRLWIND	Jun. 28, 1901	I	TURTLE
Sept. 15, 1900	I	EAGLE	Jul. 11, 1901	I	PANTHER
Sept. 28, 1900	I	RABBIT	Jul. 24, 1901	I	DEER
Oct. 11, 1900	I	TURTLE	Aug. 6, 1901	I	FLOWER
Oct. 24, 1900	I	PANTHER			

Aug. 19, 1901	I	REED	Jan. 21, 1903	I	REED
Sept. 1, 1901	I	TWINS	Feb. 3, 1903	I	TWINS
Sept. 14, 1901	I	REDBIRD	Feb. 16, 1903	I	REDBIRD
Sept. 27, 1901	I	RATTLESNAKE TOOTH	Mar. 1, 1903	I	RATTLESNAKE TOOTH
Oct. 10, 1901	I	SERPENT	Mar. 14, 1903	I	SERPENT
Oct. 23, 1901	I	FLINT	Mar. 27, 1903	I	FLINT
Nov. 5, 1901	I	RACCOON	Apr. 9, 1903	I	RACCOON
Nov. 18, 1901	I	DRAGON	Apr. 22, 1903	I	DRAGON
Dec. 1, 1901	I	HERON	May 5, 1903	I	HERON
Dec. 14, 1901	I	WOLF	May 18, 1903	I	WOLF
Dec. 27, 1901	I	HEARTH	May 31, 1903	I	HEARTH
Jan. 9, 1902	I	OWL	Jun. 13, 1903	I	OWL
Jan. 22, 1902	I	THE RIVER	Jun. 26, 1903	I	THE RIVER
Feb. 4, 1902	I	WHIRLWIND	Jul. 9, 1903	I	WHIRLWIND
Feb. 17, 1902	I	EAGLE	Jul. 22, 1903	I	EAGLE
Mar. 2, 1902	I	RABBIT	Aug. 4, 1903	I	RABBIT
Mar. 15, 1902	I	TURTLE	Aug. 17, 1903	I	TURTLE
Mar. 28, 1902	I	PANTHER	Aug. 30, 1903	I	PANTHER
Apr. 10, 1902	I	DEER	Sept. 12, 1903	I	DEER
Apr. 23, 1902	I	FLOWER	Sept. 25, 1903	I	FLOWER
May 6, 1902	I	REED	Oct. 8, 1903	I	REED
May 19, 1902	I	TWINS	Oct. 21, 1903	I	TWINS
Jun. 1, 1902	I	REDBIRD	Nov. 3, 1903	I	REDBIRD
Jun. 14, 1902	I	RATTLESNAKE TOOTH	Nov. 16, 1903	I	RATTLESNAKE TOOTH
Jun. 27, 1902	I	SERPENT	Nov. 29, 1903	I	SERPENT
Jul. 10, 1902	I	FLINT	Dec. 12, 1903	I	FLINT
Jul. 23, 1902	I	RACCOON	Dec. 25, 1903	I	RACCOON
Aug. 5, 1902	I	DRAGON	Jan. 7, 1904	I	DRAGON
Aug. 18, 1902	I	HERON	Jan. 20, 1904	I	HERON
Aug. 31, 1902	I	WOLF	Feb. 2, 1904	I	WOLF
Sept. 13, 1902	I	HEARTH	Feb. 15, 1904	I	HEARTH
Sept. 26, 1902	I	OWL	Feb. 28, 1904	I	OWL
Oct. 9, 1902	I	THE RIVER	Mar. 12, 1904	I	THE RIVER
Oct. 22, 1902	I	WHIRLWIND	Mar. 25, 1904	I	WHIRLWIND
Nov. 4, 1902	I	EAGLE	Apr. 7, 1904	I	EAGLE
Nov. 17, 1902	I	RABBIT	Apr. 20, 1904	I	RABBIT
Nov. 30, 1902	I	TURTLE	May 3, 1904	I	TURTLE
Dec. 13, 1902	I	PANTHER	May 16, 1904	I	PANTHER
Dec. 26, 1902	I	DEER	May 29, 1904	I	DEER
Jan. 8, 1903	I	FLOWER	Jun. 11, 1904	I	FLOWER

Jun. 24, 1904	I	REED
Jul. 7, 1904	I	TWINS
Jul. 20, 1904	I	REDBIRD
Aug. 2, 1904	I	RATTLESNAKE TOOTH
Aug. 15, 1904	I	SERPENT
Aug. 28, 1904	I	FLINT
Sept. 10, 1904	I	RACCOON
Sept. 23, 1904	I	DRAGON
Oct. 6, 1904	I	HERON
Oct. 19, 1904	I	WOLF
Nov. 1, 1904	I	HEARTH
Nov. 14, 1904	I	OWL
Nov. 27, 1904	I	THE RIVER
Dec. 10, 1904	I	WHIRLWIND
Dec. 23, 1904	I	EAGLE
Jan. 5, 1905	I	RABBIT
Jan. 18, 1905	I	TURTLE
Jan. 31, 1905	I	PANTHER
Feb. 13, 1905	I	DEER
Feb. 26, 1905	I	FLOWER
Mar. 11, 1905	I	REED
Mar. 24, 1905	I	TWINS
Apr. 6, 1905	I	REDBIRD
Apr. 19, 1905	I	RATTLESNAKE TOOTH
May 2, 1905	I	SERPENT
May 15, 1905	I	FLINT
May 28, 1905	I	RACCOON
Jun. 10, 1905	I	DRAGON
Jun. 23, 1905	I	HERON
Jul. 6, 1905	I	WOLF
Jul. 19, 1905	I	HEARTH
Aug. 1, 1905	I	OWL
Aug. 14, 1905	I	THE RIVER
Aug. 27, 1905	I	WHIRLWIND
Sept. 9, 1905	I	EAGLE
Sept. 22, 1905	I	RABBIT
Oct. 5, 1905	I	TURTLE
Oct. 18, 1905	I	PANTHER
Oct. 31, 1905	I	DEER
Nov. 13, 1905	I	FLOWER

Nov. 26, 1905	I	REED
Dec. 9, 1905	I	TWINS
Dec. 22, 1905	I	REDBIRD
Jan. 4, 1906	I	RATTLESNAKE TOOTH
Jan. 17, 1906	I	SERPENT
Jan. 30, 1906	I	FLINT
Feb. 12, 1906	I	RACCOON
Feb. 25, 1906	I	DRAGON
Mar. 10, 1906	I	HERON
Mar. 23, 1906	I	WOLF
Apr. 5, 1906	I	HEARTH
Apr. 18, 1906	I	OWL
May 1, 1906	I	THE RIVER
May 14, 1906	I	WHIRLWIND
May 27, 1906	I	EAGLE
Jun. 9, 1906	I	RABBIT
Jun. 22, 1906	I	TURTLE
Jul. 5, 1906	I	PANTHER
Jul. 18, 1906	I	DEER
Jul. 31, 1906	I	FLOWER
Aug. 13, 1906	I	REED
Aug. 26, 1906	I	TWINS
Sept. 8, 1906	I	REDBIRD
Sept. 21, 1906	I	RATTLESNAKE TOOTH
Oct. 4, 1906	I	SERPENT
Oct. 17, 1906	I	FLINT
Oct. 30, 1906	I	RACCOON
Nov. 12, 1906	I	DRAGON
Nov. 25, 1906	I	HERON
Dec. 8, 1906	I	WOLF
Dec. 21, 1906	I	HEARTH
Jan. 3, 1907	I	OWL
Jan. 16, 1907	I	THE RIVER
Jan. 29, 1907	I	WHIRLWIND
Feb. 11, 1907	I	EAGLE
Feb. 24, 1907	I	RABBIT
Mar. 9, 1907	I	TURTLE
Mar. 22, 1907	I	PANTHER
Apr. 4, 1907	I	DEER
Apr. 17, 1907	I	FLOWER

Apr. 30, 1907	I	REED	Oct. 1, 1908	I	REED
May 13, 1907	I	TWINS	Oct. 14, 1908	I	TWINS
May 26, 1907	I	REDBIRD	Oct. 27, 1908	I	REDBIRD
Jun. 8, 1907	I	RATTLESNAKE TOOTH	Nov. 9, 1908	I	RATTLESNAKE TOOTH
Jun. 21, 1907	I	SERPENT	Nov. 22, 1908	I	SERPENT
Jul. 4, 1907	I	FLINT	Dec. 5, 1908	I	FLINT
Jul. 17, 1907	I	RACCOON	Dec. 18, 1908	I	RACCOON
Jul. 30, 1907	I	DRAGON	Dec. 31, 1908	I	DRAGON
Aug. 12, 1907	I	HERON	Jan. 13, 1909	I	HERON
Aug. 25, 1907	I	WOLF	Jan. 26, 1909	I	WOLF
Sept. 7, 1907	I	HEARTH	Feb. 8, 1909	I	HEARTH
Sept. 20, 1907	I	OWL	Feb. 21, 1909	I	OWL
Oct. 3, 1907	I	THE RIVER	Mar. 6, 1909	I	THE RIVER
Oct. 16, 1907	I	WHIRLWIND	Mar. 19, 1909	I	WHIRLWIND
Oct. 29, 1907	I	EAGLE	Apr. 1, 1909	I	EAGLE
Nov. 11, 1907	I	RABBIT	Apr. 14, 1909	I	RABBIT
Nov. 24, 1907	I	TURTLE	Apr. 27, 1909	I	TURTLE
Dec. 7, 1907	I	PANTHER	May 10, 1909	I	PANTHER
Dec. 20, 1907	I	DEER	May 23, 1909	I	DEER
Jan. 2, 1908	I	FLOWER	Jun. 5, 1909	I	FLOWER
Jan. 15, 1908	I	REED	Jun. 18, 1909	I	REED
Jan. 28, 1908	I	TWINS	Jul. 1, 1909	I	TWINS
Feb. 10, 1908	I	REDBIRD	Jul. 14, 1909	I	REDBIRD
Feb. 23, 1908	I	RATTLESNAKE TOOTH	Jul. 27, 1909	I	RATTLESNAKE TOOTH
Mar. 7, 1908	I	SERPENT	Aug. 9, 1909	I	SERPENT
Mar. 20, 1908	I	FLINT	Aug. 22, 1909	I	FLINT
Apr. 2, 1908	I	RACCOON	Sept. 4, 1909	I	RACCOON
Apr. 15, 1908	I	DRAGON	Sept. 17, 1909	I	DRAGON
Apr. 28, 1908	I	HERON	Sept. 30, 1909	I	HERON
May 11, 1908	I	WOLF	Oct. 13, 1909	I	WOLF
May 24, 1908	I	HEARTH	Oct. 26, 1909	I	HEARTH
Jun. 6, 1908	I	OWL	Nov. 8, 1909	I	OWL
Jun. 19, 1908	I	THE RIVER	Nov. 21, 1909	I	THE RIVER
Jul. 2, 1908	I	WHIRLWIND	Dec. 4, 1909	I	WHIRLWIND
Jul. 15, 1908	I	EAGLE	Dec. 17, 1909	I	EAGLE
Jul. 28, 1908	I	RABBIT	Dec. 30, 1909	I	RABBIT
Aug. 10, 1908	I	TURTLE	Jan. 12, 1910	I	TURTLE
Aug. 23, 1908	I	PANTHER	Jan. 25, 1910	I	PANTHER
Sept. 5, 1908	I	DEER	Feb. 7, 1910	I	DEER
Sept. 18, 1908	I	FLOWER	Feb. 20, 1910	I	FLOWER

Mar. 5, 1910	I REED		Aug. 7, 1911	I REED
Mar. 18, 1910	I TWINS		Aug. 20, 1911	I TWINS
Mar. 31, 1910	I REDBIRD		Sept. 2, 1911	I REDBIRD
Apr. 13, 1910	I RATTLESNAKE TOOTH		Sept. 15, 1911	I RATTLESNAKE TOOTH
Apr. 26, 1910	I SERPENT		Sept. 28, 1911	I SERPENT
May 9, 1910	I FLINT		Oct. 11, 1911	I FLINT
May 22, 1910	I RACCOON		Oct. 24, 1911	I RACCOON
Jun. 4, 1910	I DRAGON		Nov. 6, 1911	I DRAGON
Jun. 17, 1910	I HERON		Nov. 19, 1911	I HERON
Jun. 30, 1910	I WOLF		Dec. 2, 1911	I WOLF
Jul. 13, 1910	I HEARTH		Dec. 15, 1911	I HEARTH
Jul. 26, 1910	I OWL		Dec. 28, 1911	I OWL
Aug. 8, 1910	I THE RIVER		Jan. 10, 1912	I THE RIVER
Aug. 21, 1910	I WHIRLWIND		Jan. 23, 1912	I WHIRLWIND
Sept. 3, 1910	I EAGLE		Feb. 5, 1912	I EAGLE
Sept. 16, 1910	I RABBIT		Feb. 18, 1912	I RABBIT
Sept. 29, 1910	I TURTLE		Mar. 2, 1912	I TURTLE
Oct. 12, 1910	I PANTHER		Mar. 15, 1912	I PANTHER
Oct. 25, 1910	I DEER		Mar. 28, 1912	I DEER
Nov. 7, 1910	I FLOWER		Apr. 10, 1912	I FLOWER
Nov. 20, 1910	I REED		Apr. 23, 1912	I REED
Dec. 3, 1910	I TWINS		May 6, 1912	I TWINS
Dec. 16, 1910	I REDBIRD		May 19, 1912	I REDBIRD
Dec. 29, 1910	I RATTLESNAKE TOOTH		Jun. 1, 1912	I RATTLESNAKE TOOTH
Jan. 11, 1911	I SERPENT		Jun. 14, 1912	I SERPENT
Jan. 24, 1911	I FLINT		Jun. 27, 1912	I FLINT
Feb. 6, 1911	I RACCOON		Jul. 10, 1912	I RACCOON
Feb. 19, 1911	I DRAGON		Jul. 23, 1912	I DRAGON
Mar. 4, 1911	I HERON		Aug. 5, 1912	I HERON
Mar. 17, 1911	I WOLF		Aug. 18, 1912	I WOLF
Mar. 30, 1911	I HEARTH		Aug. 31, 1912	I HEARTH
Apr. 12, 1911	I OWL		Sept. 13, 1912	I OWL
Apr. 25, 1911	I THE RIVER		Sept. 26, 1912	I THE RIVER
May 8, 1911	I WHIRLWIND		Oct. 9, 1912	I WHIRLWIND
May 21, 1911	I EAGLE		Oct. 22, 1912	I EAGLE
Jun. 3, 1911	I RABBIT		Nov. 4, 1912	I RABBIT
Jun. 16, 1911	I TURTLE		Nov. 17, 1912	I TURTLE
Jun. 29, 1911	I PANTHER		Nov. 30, 1912	I PANTHER
Jul. 12, 1911	I DEER		Dec. 13, 1912	I DEER
Jul. 25, 1911	I FLOWER		Dec. 26, 1912	I FLOWER

Jan. 8, 1913	I	REED	Jun. 12, 1914	I	REED
Jan. 21, 1913	I	TWINS	Jun. 25, 1914	I	TWINS
Feb. 3, 1913	I	REDBIRD	Jul. 8, 1914	I	REDBIRD
Feb. 16, 1913	I	RATTLESNAKE TOOTH	Jul. 21, 1914	I	RATTLESNAKE TOOTH
Mar. 1, 1913	I	SERPENT	Aug. 3, 1914	I	SERPENT
Mar. 14, 1913	I	FLINT	Aug. 16, 1914	I	FLINT
Mar. 27, 1913	I	RACCOON	Aug. 29, 1914	I	RACCOON
Apr. 9, 1913	I	DRAGON	Sept. 11, 1914	I	DRAGON
Apr. 22, 1913	I	HERON	Sept. 24, 1914	I	HERON
May 5, 1913	I	WOLF	Oct. 7, 1914	I	WOLF
May 18, 1913	I	HEARTH	Oct. 20, 1914	I	HEARTH
May 31, 1913	I	OWL	Nov. 2, 1914	I	OWL
Jun. 13, 1913	I	THE RIVER	Nov. 15, 1914	I	THE RIVER
Jun. 26, 1913	I	WHIRLWIND	Nov. 28, 1914	I	WHIRLWIND
Jul. 9, 1913	I	EAGLE	Dec. 11, 1914	I	EAGLE
Jul. 22, 1913	I	RABBIT	Dec. 24, 1914	I	RABBIT
Aug. 4, 1913	I	TURTLE	Jan. 6, 1915	I	TURTLE
Aug. 17, 1913	I	PANTHER	Jan. 19, 1915	I	PANTHER
Aug. 30, 1913	I	DEER	Feb. 1, 1915	I	DEER
Sept. 12, 1913	I	FLOWER	Feb. 14, 1915	I	FLOWER
Sept. 25, 1913	I	REED	Feb. 27, 1915	I	REED
Oct. 8, 1913	I	TWINS	Mar. 12, 1915	I	TWINS
Oct. 21, 1913	I	REDBIRD	Mar. 25, 1915	I	REDBIRD
Nov. 3, 1913	I	RATTLESNAKE TOOTH	Apr. 7, 1915	I	RATTLESNAKE TOOTH
Nov. 16, 1913	I	SERPENT	Apr. 20, 1915	I	SERPENT
Nov. 29, 1913	I	FLINT	May 3, 1915	I	FLINT
Dec. 12, 1913	I	RACCOON	May 16, 1915	I	RACCOON
Dec. 25, 1913	I	DRAGON	May 29, 1915	I	DRAGON
Jan. 7, 1914	I	HERON	Jun. 11, 1915	I	HERON
Jan. 20, 1914	I	WOLF	Jun. 24, 1915	I	WOLF
Feb. 2, 1914	I	HEARTH	Jul. 7, 1915	I	HEARTH
Feb. 15, 1914	I	OWL	Jul. 20, 1915	I	OWL
Feb. 28, 1914	I	THE RIVER	Aug. 2, 1915	I	THE RIVER
Mar. 13, 1914	I	WHIRLWIND	Aug. 15, 1915	I	WHIRLWIND
Mar. 26, 1914	I	EAGLE	Aug. 28, 1915	I	EAGLE
Apr. 8, 1914	I	RABBIT	Sept. 10, 1915	I	RABBIT
Apr. 21, 1914	I	TURTLE	Sept. 23, 1915	I	TURTLE
May 4, 1914	I	PANTHER	Oct. 6, 1915	I	PANTHER
May 17, 1914	I	DEER	Oct. 19, 1915	I	DEER
May 30, 1914	I	FLOWER	Nov. 1, 1915	I	FLOWER

Nov. 14, 1915	I	REED
Nov. 27, 1915	I	TWINS
Dec. 10, 1915	I	REDBIRD
Dec. 23, 1915	I	RATTLESNAKE TOOTH
Jan. 5, 1916	I	SERPENT
Jan. 18, 1916	I	FLINT
Jan. 31, 1916	I	RACCOON
Feb. 13, 1916	I	DRAGON
Feb. 26, 1916	I	HERON
Mar. 10, 1916	I	WOLF
Mar. 23, 1916	I	HEARTH
Apr. 5, 1916	I	OWL
Apr. 18, 1916	I	THE RIVER
May 1, 1916	I	WHIRLWIND
May 14, 1916	I	EAGLE
May 27, 1916	I	RABBIT
Jun. 9, 1916	I	TURTLE
Jun. 22, 1916	I	PANTHER
Jul. 5, 1916	I	DEER
Jul. 18, 1916	I	FLOWER
Jul 31, 1916	I	REED
Aug. 13, 1916	I	TWINS
Aug. 26, 1916	I	REDBIRD
Sept. 8, 1916	I	RATTLESNAKE TOOTH
Sept. 21, 1916	I	SERPENT
Oct. 4, 1916	I	FLINT
Oct. 17, 1916	I	RACCOON
Oct. 30, 1916	I	DRAGON
Nov. 12, 1916	I	HERON
Nov. 25, 1916	I	WOLF
Dec. 8, 1916	I	HEARTH
Dec. 21, 1916	I	OWL
Jan. 3, 1917	I	THE RIVER
Jan. 16, 1917	I	WHIRLWIND
Jan. 29, 1917	I	EAGLE
Feb. 11, 1917	I	RABBIT
Feb. 24, 1917	I	TURTLE
Mar. 9, 1917	I	PANTHER
Mar. 22, 1917	I	DEER
Apr. 4, 1917	I	FLOWER

Apr. 17, 1917	I	REED
Apr. 30, 1917	I	TWINS
May 13, 1917	I	REDBIRD
May 26, 1917	I	RATTLESNAKE TOOTH
Jun. 8, 1917	I	SERPENT
Jun. 21, 1917	I	FLINT
Jul. 4, 1917	I	RACCOON
Jul. 17, 1917	I	DRAGON
Jul. 30, 1917	I	HERON
Aug. 12, 1917	I	WOLF
Aug. 25, 1917	I	HEARTH
Sept. 7, 1917	I	OWL
Sept. 20, 1917	I	THE RIVER
Oct. 3, 1917	I	WHIRLWIND
Oct. 16, 1917	I	EAGLE
Oct. 29, 1917	I	RABBIT
Nov. 11, 1917	I	TURTLE
Nov. 24, 1917	I	PANTHER
Dec. 7, 1917	I	DEER
Dec. 20, 1917	I	FLOWER
Jan. 2, 1918	I	REED
Jan. 15, 1918	I	TWINS
Jan. 28, 1918	I	REDBIRD
Feb. 10, 1918	I	RATTLESNAKE TOOTH
Feb. 23, 1918	I	SERPENT
Mar. 8, 1918	I	FLINT
Mar. 21, 1918	I	RACCOON
Apr. 3, 1918	I	DRAGON
Apr. 16, 1918	I	HERON
Apr. 29, 1918	I	WOLF
May 12, 1918	I	HEARTH
May 25, 1918	I	OWL
Jun. 7, 1918	I	THE RIVER
Jun. 20, 1918	I	WHIRLWIND
Jul. 3, 1918	I	EAGLE
Jul. 16, 1918	I	RABBIT
Jul. 29, 1918	I	TURTLE
Aug. 11, 1918	I	PANTHER
Aug. 24, 1918	I	DEER
Sept. 6, 1918	I	FLOWER

Sept. 19, 1918	REED	Feb. 21, 1920	REED
Oct. 2, 1918	TWINS	Mar. 5, 1920	TWINS
Oct. 15, 1918	REDBIRD	Mar. 18, 1920	REDBIRD
Oct. 28, 1918	RATTLESNAKE TOOTH	Mar. 31, 1920	RATTLESNAKE TOOTH
Nov. 10, 1918	SERPENT	Apr. 13, 1920	SERPENT
Nov. 23, 1918	FLINT	Apr. 26, 1920	FLINT
Dec. 6, 1918	RACCOON	May 9, 1920	RACCOON
Dec. 19, 1918	DRAGON	May 22, 1920	DRAGON
Jan. 1, 1919	HERON	Jun. 4, 1920	HERON
Jan. 14, 1919	WOLF	Jun. 17, 1920	WOLF
Jan. 27, 1919	HEARTH	Jun. 30, 1920	HEARTH
Feb. 9, 1919	OWL	Jul. 13, 1920	OWL
Feb. 22, 1919	THE RIVER	Jul. 26, 1920	THE RIVER
Mar. 7, 1919	WHIRLWIND	Aug. 8, 1920	WHIRLWIND
Mar. 20, 1919	EAGLE	Aug. 21, 1920	EAGLE
Apr. 2, 1919	RABBIT	Sept. 3, 1920	RABBIT
Apr. 15, 1919	TURTLE	Sept. 16, 1920	TURTLE
Apr. 28, 1919	PANTHER	Sept. 29, 1920	PANTHER
May 11, 1919	DEER	Oct. 12, 1920	DEER
May 24, 1919	FLOWER	Oct. 25, 1920	FLOWER
Jun. 6, 1919	REED	Nov. 7, 1920	REED
Jun. 19, 1919	TWINS	Nov. 20, 1920	TWINS
Jul. 2, 1919	REDBIRD	Dec. 3, 1920	REDBIRD
Jul. 15, 1919	RATTLESNAKE TOOTH	Dec. 16, 1920	RATTLESNAKE TOOTH
Jul. 28, 1919	SERPENT	Dec. 29, 1920	SERPENT
Aug. 10, 1919	FLINT	Jan. 11, 1921	FLINT
Aug. 23, 1919	RACCOON	Jan. 24, 1921	RACCOON
Sept. 5, 1919	DRAGON	Feb. 6, 1921	DRAGON
Sept. 18, 1919	HERON	Feb. 19, 1921	HERON
Oct. 1, 1919	WOLF	Mar. 4, 1921	WOLF
Oct. 14, 1919	HEARTH	Mar. 17, 1921	HEARTH
Oct. 27, 1919	OWL	Mar. 30, 1921	OWL
Nov. 9, 1919	THE RIVER	Apr. 12, 1921	THE RIVER
Nov. 22, 1919	WHIRLWIND	Apr. 25, 1921	WHIRLWIND
Dec. 5, 1919	EAGLE	May 8, 1921	EAGLE
Dec. 18, 1919	RABBIT	May 21, 1921	RABBIT
Dec. 31, 1919	TURTLE	Jun. 3, 1921	TURTLE
Jan. 13, 1920	PANTHER	Jun. 16, 1921	PANTHER
Jan. 26, 1920	DEER	Jun. 29, 1921	DEER
Feb. 8, 1920	FLOWER	Jul. 12, 1921	FLOWER

Jul. 25, 1921	I	REED	Dec. 27, 1922	I	REED
Aug. 7, 1921	I	TWINS	Jan. 9, 1923	I	TWINS
Aug. 20, 1921	I	REDBIRD	Jan. 22, 1923	I	REDBIRD
Sept. 2, 1921	I	RATTLESNAKE TOOTH	Feb. 4, 1923	I	RATTLESNAKE TOOTH
Sept. 15, 1921	I	SERPENT	Feb. 17, 1923	I	SERPENT
Sept. 28, 1921	I	FLINT	Mar. 2, 1923	I	FLINT
Oct. 11, 1921	I	RACCOON	Mar. 15, 1923	I	RACCOON
Oct. 24, 1921	I	DRAGON	Mar. 28, 1923	I	DRAGON
Nov. 6, 1921	I	HERON	Apr. 10, 1923	I	HERON
Nov. 19, 1921	I	WOLF	Apr. 23, 1923	I	WOLF
Dec. 2, 1921	I	HEARTH	May 6, 1923	I	HEARTH
Dec. 15, 1921	I	OWL	May 19, 1923	I	OWL
Dec. 28, 1921	I	THE RIVER	Jun. 1, 1923	I	THE RIVER
Jan. 10, 1922	I	WHIRLWIND	Jun. 14, 1923	I	WHIRLWIND
Jan. 23, 1922	I	EAGLE	Jun. 27, 1923	I	EAGLE
Feb. 5, 1922	I	RABBIT	Jul. 10, 1923	I	RABBIT
Feb. 18, 1922	I	TURTLE	Jul. 23, 1923	I	TURTLE
Mar. 3, 1922	I	PANTHER	Aug. 5, 1923	I	PANTHER
Mar. 16, 1922	I	DEER	Aug. 18, 1923	I	DEER
Mar. 29, 1922	I	FLOWER	Aug. 31, 1923	I	FLOWER
Apr. 11, 1922	I	REED	Sept. 13, 1923	I	REED
Apr. 24, 1922	I	TWINS	Sept. 26, 1923	I	TWINS
May 7, 1922	I	REDBIRD	Oct. 9, 1923	I	REDBIRD
May 20, 1922	I	RATTLESNAKE TOOTH	Oct. 22, 1923	I	RATTLESNAKE TOOTH
Jun. 2, 1922	I	SERPENT	Nov. 4, 1923	I	SERPENT
Jun. 15, 1922	I	FLINT	Nov. 17, 1923	I	FLINT
Jun. 28, 1922	I	RACCOON	Nov. 30, 1923	I	RACCOON
Jul. 11, 1922	I	DRAGON	Dec. 13, 1923	I	DRAGON
Jul. 24, 1922	I	HERON	Dec. 26, 1923	I	HERON
Aug. 6, 1922	I	WOLF	Jan. 8, 1924	I	WOLF
Aug. 19, 1922	I	HEARTH	Jan. 21, 1924	I	HEARTH
Sept. 1, 1922	I	OWL	Feb. 3, 1924	I	OWL
Sept. 14, 1922	I	THE RIVER	Feb. 16, 1924	I	THE RIVER
Sept. 27, 1922	I	WHIRLWIND	Feb. 29, 1924	I	WHIRLWIND
Oct. 10, 1922	I	EAGLE	Mar. 13, 1924	I	EAGLE
Oct. 23, 1922	I	RABBIT	Mar. 26, 1924	I	RABBIT
Nov. 5, 1922	I	TURTLE	Apr. 8, 1924	I	TURTLE
Nov. 18, 1922	I	PANTHER	Apr. 21, 1924	I	PANTHER
Dec. 1, 1922	I	DEER	May 4, 1924	I	DEER
Dec. 14, 1922	I	FLOWER	May 17, 1924	I	FLOWER

May 30, 1924	I	REED	Nov. 1, 1925	I	REED
Jun. 12, 1924	I	TWINS	Nov. 14, 1925	I	TWINS
Jun. 25, 1924	I	REDBIRD	Nov. 27, 1925	I	REDBIRD
Jul. 8, 1924	I	RATTLESNAKE TOOTH	Dec. 10, 1925	I	RATTLESNAKE TOOTH
Jul. 21, 1924	I	SERPENT	Dec. 23, 1925	I	SERPENT
Aug. 3, 1924	I	FLINT	Jan. 5, 1926	I	FLINT
Aug. 16, 1924	I	RACCOON	Jan. 18, 1926	I	RACCOON
Aug. 29, 1924	I	DRAGON	Jan. 31, 1926	I	DRAGON
Sept. 11, 1924	I	HERON	Feb. 13, 1926	I	HERON
Sept. 24, 1924	I	WOLF	Feb. 26, 1926	I	WOLF
Oct. 7, 1924	I	HEARTH	Mar. 11, 1926	I	HEARTH
Oct. 20, 1924	I	OWL	Mar. 24, 1926	I	OWL
Nov. 2, 1924	I	THE RIVER	Apr. 6, 1926	I	THE RIVER
Nov. 15, 1924	I	WHIRLWIND	Apr. 19, 1926	I	WHIRLWIND
Nov. 28, 1924	I	EAGLE	May 2, 1926	I	EAGLE
Dec. 11, 1924	I	RABBIT	May 15, 1926	I	RABBIT
Dec. 24, 1924	I	TURTLE	May 28, 1926	I	TURTLE
Jan. 6, 1925	I	PANTHER	Jun. 10, 1926	I	PANTHER
Jan. 19, 1925	I	DEER	Jun. 23, 1926	I	DEER
Feb. 1, 1925	I	FLOWER	Jul. 6, 1926	I	FLOWER
Feb. 14, 1925	I	REED	Jul.19, 1926	I	REED
Feb. 27, 1925	I	TWINS	Aug. 1, 1926	I	TWINS
Mar. 12, 1925	I	REDBIRD	Aug. 14, 1926	I	REDBIRD
Mar. 25, 1925	I	RATTLESNAKE TOOTH	Aug. 27, 1926	I	RATTLESNAKE TOOTH
Apr. 7, 1925	I	SERPENT	Sept. 9, 1926	I	SERPENT
Apr. 20, 1925	I	FLINT	Sept. 22, 1926	I	FLINT
May 3, 1925	I	RACCOON	Oct. 5, 1926	I	RACCOON
May 16, 1925	I	DRAGON	Oct. 18, 1926	I	DRAGON
May 29, 1925	I	HERON	Oct. 31, 1926	I	HERON
Jun. 11, 1925	I	WOLF	Nov. 13, 1926	I	WOLF
Jun. 24, 1925	I	HEARTH	Nov. 26, 1926	I	HEARTH
Jul. 7, 1925	I	OWL	Dec. 9, 1926	I	OWL
Jul. 20, 1925	I	THE RIVER	Dec. 22, 1926	I	THE RIVER
Aug. 2, 1925	I	WHIRLWIND	Jan. 4, 1927	I	WHIRLWIND
Aug. 15, 1925	I	EAGLE	Jan. 17, 1927	I	EAGLE
Aug. 28, 1925	I	RABBIT	Jan. 30, 1927	I	RABBIT
Sept. 10, 1925	I	TURTLE	Feb. 12, 1927	I	TURTLE
Sept. 23, 1925	I	PANTHER	Feb. 25, 1927	I	PANTHER
Oct. 6, 1925	I	DEER	Mar. 10, 1927	I	DEER
Oct. 19, 1925	I	FLOWER	Mar. 23, 1927	I	FLOWER

Apr. 5, 1927	I	REED	Sept. 6, 1928	I	REED
Apr. 18, 1927	I	TWINS	Sept. 19, 1928	I	TWINS
May 1, 1927	I	REDBIRD	Oct. 2, 1928	I	REDBIRD
May 14, 1927	I	RATTLESNAKE TOOTH	Oct. 15, 1928	I	RATTLESNAKE TOOTH
May 27, 1927	I	SERPENT	Oct. 28, 1928	I	SERPENT
Jun. 9, 1927	I	FLINT	Nov. 10, 1928	I	FLINT
Jun. 22, 1927	I	RACCOON	Nov. 23, 1928	I	RACCOON
Jul. 5, 1927	I	DRAGON	Dec. 6, 1928	I	DRAGON
Jul. 18, 1927	I	HERON	Dec. 19, 1928	I	HERON
Jul. 31, 1927	I	WOLF	Jan. 1, 1929	I	WOLF
Aug. 13, 1927	I	HEARTH	Jan. 14, 1929	I	HEARTH
Aug. 26, 1927	I	OWL	Jan. 27, 1929	I	OWL
Sept. 8, 1927	I	THE RIVER	Feb. 9, 1929	I	THE RIVER
Sept. 21, 1927	I	WHIRLWIND	Feb. 22, 1929	I	WHIRLWIND
Oct. 4, 1927	I	EAGLE	Mar. 7, 1929	I	EAGLE
Oct. 17, 1927	I	RABBIT	Mar. 20, 1929	I	RABBIT
Oct. 30, 1927	I	TURTLE	Apr. 2, 1929	I	TURTLE
Nov. 12, 1927	I	PANTHER	Apr. 15, 1929	I	PANTHER
Nov. 25, 1927	I	DEER	Apr. 28, 1929	I	DEER
Dec. 8, 1927	I	FLOWER	May 11, 1929	I	FLOWER
Dec. 21, 1927	I	REED	May 24, 1929	I	REED
Jan. 3, 1928	I	TWINS	Jun. 6, 1929	I	TWINS
Jan. 16, 1928	I	REDBIRD	Jun. 19, 1929	I	REDBIRD
Jan. 29, 1928	I	RATTLESNAKE TOOTH	Jul. 2, 1929	I	RATTLESNAKE TOOTH
Feb. 11, 1928	I	SERPENT	Jul. 15, 1929	I	SERPENT
Feb. 24, 1928	I	FLINT	Jul. 28, 1929	I	FLINT
Mar. 8, 1928	I	RACCOON	Aug. 10, 1929	I	RACCOON
Mar. 21, 1928	I	DRAGON	Aug. 23, 1929	I	DRAGON
Apr. 3, 1928	I	HERON	Sept. 5, 1929	I	HERON
Apr. 16, 1928	I	WOLF	Sept. 18, 1929	I	WOLF
Apr. 29, 1928	I	HEARTH	Oct. 1, 1929	I	HEARTH
May 12, 1928	I	OWL	Oct. 14, 1929	I	OWL
May 25, 1928	I	THE RIVER	Oct. 27, 1929	I	THE RIVER
Jun. 7, 1928	I	WHIRLWIND	Nov. 9, 1929	I	WHIRLWIND
Jun. 20, 1928	I	EAGLE	Nov. 22, 1929	I	EAGLE
Jul. 3, 1928	I	RABBIT	Dec. 5, 1929	I	RABBIT
Jul. 16, 1928	I	TURTLE	Dec. 18, 1929	I	TURTLE
Jul. 29, 1928	I	PANTHER	Dec. 31, 1929	I	PANTHER
Aug. 11, 1928	I	DEER	Jan. 13, 1930	I	DEER
Aug. 24, 1928	I	FLOWER	Jan. 26, 1930	I	FLOWER

Feb. 8, 1930	I	REED
Feb. 21, 1930	I	TWINS
Mar. 6, 1930	I	REDBIRD
Mar. 19, 1930	I	RATTLESNAKE TOOTH
Apr. 1, 1930	I	SERPENT
Apr. 14, 1930	I	FLINT
Apr. 27, 1930	I	RACCOON
May 10, 1930	I	DRAGON
May 23, 1930	I	HERON
Jun. 5, 1930	I	WOLF
Jun. 18, 1930	I	HEARTH
Jul. 1, 1930	I	OWL
Jul. 14, 1930	I	THE RIVER
Jul. 27, 1930	I	WHIRLWIND
Aug. 9, 1930	I	EAGLE
Aug. 22, 1930	I	RABBIT
Sept. 4, 1930	I	TURTLE
Sept. 17, 1930	I	PANTHER
Sept. 30, 1930	I	DEER
Oct. 13, 1930	I	FLOWER
Oct. 26, 1930	I	REED
Nov. 8, 1930	I	TWINS
Nov. 21, 1930	I	REDBIRD
Dec. 4, 1930	I	RATTLESNAKE TOOTH
Dec. 17, 1930	I	SERPENT
Dec. 30, 1930	I	FLINT
Jan. 12, 1931	I	RACCOON
Jan. 25, 1931	I	DRAGON
Feb. 7, 1931	I	HERON
Feb. 20, 1931	I	WOLF
Mar. 5, 1931	I	HEARTH
Mar. 18, 1931	I	OWL
Mar. 31, 1931	I	THE RIVER
Apr. 13, 1931	I	WHIRLWIND
Apr. 26, 1931	I	EAGLE
May 9, 1931	I	RABBIT
May 22, 1931	I	TURTLE
Jun. 4, 1931	I	PANTHER
Jun. 17, 1931	I	DEER
Jun. 30, 1931	I	FLOWER

Jul. 13, 1931	I	REED
Jul. 26, 1931	I	TWINS
Aug. 8, 1931	I	REDBIRD
Aug. 21, 1931	I	RATTLESNAKE TOOTH
Sept. 3, 1931	I	SERPENT
Sept. 16, 1931	I	FLINT
Sept. 29, 1931	I	RACCOON
Oct. 12, 1931	I	DRAGON
Oct. 25, 1931	I	HERON
Nov. 7, 1931	I	WOLF
Nov. 20, 1931	I	HEARTH
Dec. 3, 1931	I	OWL
Dec. 16, 1931	I	THE RIVER
Dec. 29, 1931	I	WHIRLWIND
Jan. 11, 1932	I	EAGLE
Jan. 24, 1932	I	RABBIT
Feb. 6, 1932	I	TURTLE
Feb. 19, 1932	I	PANTHER
Mar. 3, 1932	I	DEER
Mar. 16, 1932	I	FLOWER
Mar. 29, 1932	I	REED
Apr. 11, 1932	I	TWINS
Apr. 24, 1932	I	REDBIRD
May 7, 1932	I	RATTLESNAKE TOOTH
May 20, 1932	I	SERPENT
Jun. 2, 1932	I	FLINT
Jun. 15, 1932	I	RACCOON
Jun. 28, 1932	I	DRAGON
Jul. 11, 1932	I	HERON
Jul. 24, 1932	I	WOLF
Aug. 6, 1932	I	HEARTH
Aug. 19, 1932	I	OWL
Sept. 1, 1932	I	THE RIVER
Sept. 14, 1932	I	WHIRLWIND
Sept. 27, 1932	I	EAGLE
Oct. 10, 1932	I	RABBIT
Oct. 23, 1932	I	TURTLE
Nov. 5, 1932	I	PANTHER
Nov. 18, 1932	I	DEER
Dec. 1, 1932	I	FLOWER

Dec. 14, 1932	I	REED	May 18, 1934	I	REED
Dec. 27, 1932	I	TWINS	May 31, 1934	I	TWINS
Jan. 9, 1933	I	REDBIRD	Jun. 13, 1934	I	REDBIRD
Jan. 22, 1933	I	RATTLESNAKE TOOTH	Jun. 26, 1934	I	RATTLESNAKE TOOTH
Feb. 4, 1933	I	SERPENT	Jul. 9, 1934	I	SERPENT
Feb. 17, 1933	I	FLINT	Jul. 22, 1934	I	FLINT
Mar. 2, 1933	I	RACCOON	Aug. 4, 1934	I	RACCOON
Mar. 15, 1933	I	DRAGON	Aug. 17, 1934	I	DRAGON
Mar. 28, 1933	I	HERON	Aug. 30, 1934	I	HERON
Apr. 10, 1933	I	WOLF	Sept. 12, 1934	I	WOLF
Apr. 23, 1933	I	HEARTH	Sept. 25, 1934	I	HEARTH
May 6, 1933	I	OWL	Oct. 8, 1934	I	OWL
May 19, 1933	I	THE RIVER	Oct. 21, 1934	I	THE RIVER
Jun. 1, 1933	I	WHIRLWIND	Nov. 3, 1934	I	WHIRLWIND
Jun. 14, 1933	I	EAGLE	Nov. 16, 1934	I	EAGLE
Jun. 27, 1933	I	RABBIT	Nov. 29, 1934	I	RABBIT
Jul. 10, 1933	I	TURTLE	Dec. 12, 1934	I	TURTLE
Jul. 23, 1933	I	PANTHER	Dec. 25, 1934	I	PANTHER
Aug. 5, 1933	I	DEER	Jan. 7, 1935	I	DEER
Aug. 18, 1933	I	FLOWER	Jan. 20, 1935	I	FLOWER
Aug. 31, 1933	I	REED	Feb. 2, 1935	I	REED
Sept. 13, 1933	I	TWINS	Feb. 15, 1935	I	TWINS
Sept. 26, 1933	I	REDBIRD	Feb. 28, 1935	I	REDBIRD
Oct. 9, 1933	I	RATTLESNAKE TOOTH	Mar. 13, 1935	I	RATTLESNAKE TOOTH
Oct. 22, 1933	I	SERPENT	Mar. 26, 1935	I	SERPENT
Nov. 4, 1933	I	FLINT	Apr. 8, 1935	I	FLINT
Nov. 17, 1933	I	RACCOON	Apr. 21, 1935	I	RACCOON
Nov. 30, 1933	I	DRAGON	May 4, 1935	I	DRAGON
Dec. 13, 1933	I	HERON	May 17, 1935	I	HERON
Dec. 26, 1933	I	WOLF	May 30, 1935	I	WOLF
Jan. 8, 1934	I	HEARTH	Jun. 12, 1935	I	HEARTH
Jan. 21, 1934	I	OWL	Jun. 25, 1935	I	OWL
Feb. 3, 1934	I	THE RIVER	Jul. 8, 1935	I	THE RIVER
Feb. 16, 1934	I	WHIRLWIND	Jul. 21, 1935	I	WHIRLWIND
Mar. 1, 1934	I	EAGLE	Aug. 3, 1935	I	EAGLE
Mar. 14, 1934	I	RABBIT	Aug. 16, 1935	I	RABBIT
Mar. 27, 1934	I	TURTLE	Aug. 29, 1935	I	TURTLE
Apr. 9, 1934	I	PANTHER	Sept. 11, 1935	I	PANTHER
Apr. 22, 1934	I	DEER	Sept. 24, 1935	I	DEER
May 5, 1934	I	FLOWER	Oct. 7, 1935	I	FLOWER

Oct. 20, 1935	I	REED	Mar. 23, 1937	I	REED
Nov. 2, 1935	I	TWINS	Apr. 5, 1937	I	TWINS
Nov. 15, 1935	I	REDBIRD	Apr. 18, 1937	I	REDBIRD
Nov. 28, 1935	I	RATTLESNAKE TOOTH	May 1, 1937	I	RATTLESNAKE TOOTH
Dec. 11, 1935	I	SERPENT	May 14, 1937	I	SERPENT
Dec. 24, 1935	I	FLINT	May 27, 1937	I	FLINT
Jan. 6, 1936	I	RACCOON	Jun. 9, 1937	I	RACCOON
Jan. 19, 1936	I	DRAGON	Jun. 22, 1937	I	DRAGON
Feb. 1, 1936	I	HERON	Jul. 5, 1937	I	HERON
Feb. 14, 1936	I	WOLF	Jul. 18, 1937	I	WOLF
Feb. 27, 1936	I	HEARTH	Jul. 31, 1937	I	HEARTH
Mar. 11, 1936	I	OWL	Aug. 13, 1937	I	OWL
Mar. 24, 1936	I	THE RIVER	Aug. 26, 1937	I	THE RIVER
Apr. 6, 1936	I	WHIRLWIND	Sept. 8, 1937	I	WHIRLWIND
Apr. 19, 1936	I	EAGLE	Sept. 21, 1937	I	EAGLE
May 2, 1936	I	RABBIT	Oct. 4, 1937	I	RABBIT
May 15, 1936	I	TURTLE	Oct. 17, 1937	I	TURTLE
May 28, 1936	I	PANTHER	Oct. 30, 1937	I	PANTHER
Jun. 10, 1936	I	DEER	Nov. 12, 1937	I	DEER
Jun. 23, 1936	I	FLOWER	Nov. 25, 1937	I	FLOWER
Jul. 6, 1936	I	REED	Dec. 8, 1937	I	REED
Jul. 19, 1936	I	TWINS	Dec. 21, 1937	I	TWINS
Aug. 1, 1936	I	REDBIRD	Jan. 3, 1938	I	REDBIRD
Aug. 14, 1936	I	RATTLESNAKE TOOTH	Jan. 16, 1938	I	RATTLESNAKE TOOTH
Aug. 27, 1936	I	SERPENT	Jan. 29, 1938	I	SERPENT
Sept. 9, 1936	I	FLINT	Feb. 11, 1938	I	FLINT
Sept. 22, 1936	I	RACCOON	Feb. 24, 1938	I	RACCOON
Oct. 5, 1936	I	DRAGON	Mar. 9, 1938	I	DRAGON
Oct. 18, 1936	I	HERON	Mar. 22, 1938	I	HERON
Oct. 31, 1936	I	WOLF	Apr. 4, 1938	I	WOLF
Nov. 13, 1936	I	HEARTH	Apr. 17, 1938	I	HEARTH
Nov. 26, 1936	I	OWL	Apr. 30, 1938	I	OWL
Dec. 9, 1936	I	THE RIVER	May 13, 1938	I	THE RIVER
Dec. 22, 1936	I	WHIRLWIND	May 26, 1938	I	WHIRLWIND
Jan. 4, 1937	I	EAGLE	Jun. 8, 1938	I	EAGLE
Jan. 17, 1937	I	RABBIT	Jun. 21, 1938	I	RABBIT
Jan. 30, 1937	I	TURTLE	Jul. 4, 1938	I	TURTLE
Feb. 12, 1937	I	PANTHER	Jul. 17, 1938	I	PANTHER
Feb. 25, 1937	I	DEER	Jul. 30, 1938	I	DEER
Mar. 10, 1937	I	FLOWER	Aug. 12, 1938	I	FLOWER

Aug. 25, 1938	I	REED	Jan. 27, 1940	I	REED
Sept. 7, 1938	I	TWINS	Feb. 9, 1940	I	TWINS
Sept. 20, 1938	I	REDBIRD	Feb. 22, 1940	I	REDBIRD
Oct. 3, 1938	I	RATTLESNAKE TOOTH	Mar. 6, 1940	I	RATTLESNAKE TOOTH
Oct. 16, 1938	I	SERPENT	Mar. 19, 1940	I	SERPENT
Oct. 29, 1938	I	FLINT	Apr. 1, 1940	I	FLINT
Nov. 11, 1938	I	RACCOON	Apr. 14, 1940	I	RACCOON
Nov. 24, 1938	I	DRAGON	Apr. 27, 1940	I	DRAGON
Dec. 7, 1938	I	HERON	May 10, 1940	I	HERON
Dec. 20, 1938	I	WOLF	May 23, 1940	I	WOLF
Jan. 2, 1939	I	HEARTH	Jun. 5, 1940	I	HEARTH
Jan. 15, 1939	I	OWL	Jun. 18, 1940	I	OWL
Jan. 28, 1939	I	THE RIVER	Jul. 1, 1940	I	THE RIVER
Feb. 10, 1939	I	WHIRLWIND	Jul. 14, 1940	I	WHIRLWIND
Feb. 23, 1939	I	EAGLE	Jul. 27, 1940	I	EAGLE
Mar. 8, 1939	I	RABBIT	Aug. 9, 1940	I	RABBIT
Mar. 21, 1939	I	TURTLE	Aug. 22, 1940	I	TURTLE
Apr. 3, 1939	I	PANTHER	Sept. 4, 1940	I	PANTHER
Apr. 16, 1939	I	DEER	Sept. 17, 1940	I	DEER
Apr. 29, 1939	I	FLOWER	Sept. 30, 1940	I	FLOWER
May 12, 1939	I	REED	Oct. 13, 1940	I	REED
May 25, 1939	I	TWINS	Oct. 26, 1940	I	TWINS
Jun. 7, 1939	I	REDBIRD	Nov. 8, 1940	I	REDBIRD
Jun. 20, 1939	I	RATTLESNAKE TOOTH	Nov. 21, 1940	I	RATTLESNAKE TOOTH
Jul. 3, 1939	I	SERPENT	Dec. 4, 1940	I	SERPENT
Jul. 16, 1939	I	FLINT	Dec. 17, 1940	I	FLINT
Jul. 29, 1939	I	RACCOON	Dec. 30, 1940	I	RACCOON
Aug. 11, 1939	I	DRAGON	Jan. 12, 1941	I	DRAGON
Aug. 24, 1939	I	HERON	Jan. 25, 1941	I	HERON
Sept. 6, 1939	I	WOLF	Feb. 7, 1941	I	WOLF
Sept. 19, 1939	I	HEARTH	Feb. 20, 1941	I	HEARTH
Oct. 2, 1939	I	OWL	Mar. 5, 1941	I	OWL
Oct. 15, 1939	I	THE RIVER	Mar. 18, 1941	I	THE RIVER
Oct. 28, 1939	I	WHIRLWIND	Mar. 31, 1941	I	WHIRLWIND
Nov. 10, 1939	I	EAGLE	Apr. 13, 1941	I	EAGLE
Nov. 23, 1939	I	RABBIT	Apr. 26, 1941	I	RABBIT
Dec. 6, 1939	I	TURTLE	May 9, 1941	I	TURTLE
Dec. 19, 1939	I	PANTHER	May 22, 1941	I	PANTHER
Jan. 1, 1940	I	DEER	Jun. 4, 1941	I	DEER
Jan. 14, 1940	I	FLOWER	Jun. 17, 1941	I	FLOWER

Jun. 30, 1941	I	REED	Dec. 2, 1942	I	REED
Jul. 13, 1941	I	TWINS	Dec. 15, 1942	I	TWINS
Jul. 26, 1941	I	REDBIRD	Dec. 28, 1942	I	REDBIRD
Aug. 8, 1941	I	RATTLESNAKE TOOTH	Jan. 10, 1943	I	RATTLESNAKE TOOTH
Aug. 21, 1941	I	SERPENT	Jan. 23, 1943	I	SERPENT
Sept. 3, 1941	I	FLINT	Feb. 5, 1943	I	FLINT
Sept. 16, 1941	I	RACCOON	Feb. 18, 1943	I	RACCOON
Sept. 29, 1941	I	DRAGON	Mar. 3, 1943	I	DRAGON
Oct. 12, 1941	I	HERON	Mar. 16, 1943	I	HERON
Oct. 25, 1941	I	WOLF	Mar. 29, 1943	I	WOLF
Nov. 7, 1941	I	HEARTH	Apr. 11, 1943	I	HEARTH
Nov. 20, 1941	I	OWL	Apr. 24, 1943	I	OWL
Dec. 3, 1941	I	THE RIVER	May 7, 1943	I	THE RIVER
Dec. 16, 1941	I	WHIRLWIND	May 20, 1943	I	WHIRLWIND
Dec. 29, 1941	I	EAGLE	Jun. 2, 1943	I	EAGLE
Jan. 11, 1942	I	RABBIT	Jun. 15, 1943	I	RABBIT
Jan. 24, 1942	I	TURTLE	Jun. 28, 1943	I	TURTLE
Feb. 6, 1942	I	PANTHER	Jul. 11, 1943	I	PANTHER
Feb. 19, 1942	I	DEER	Jul. 24, 1943	I	DEER
Mar. 4, 1942	I	FLOWER	Aug. 6, 1943	I	FLOWER
Mar. 17, 1942	I	REED	Aug. 19, 1943	I	REED
Mar. 30, 1942	I	TWINS	Sept. 1, 1943	I	TWINS
Apr. 12, 1942	I	REDBIRD	Sept. 14, 1943	I	REDBIRD
Apr. 25, 1942	I	RATTLESNAKE TOOTH	Sept. 27, 1943	I	RATTLESNAKE TOOTH
May 8, 1942	I	SERPENT	Oct. 10, 1943	I	SERPENT
May 21, 1942	I	FLINT	Oct. 23, 1943	I	FLINT
Jun. 3, 1942	I	RACCOON	Nov. 5, 1943	I	RACCOON
Jun. 16, 1942	I	DRAGON	Nov. 18, 1943	I	DRAGON
Jun. 29, 1942	I	HERON	Dec. 1, 1943	I	HERON
Jul. 12, 1942	I	WOLF	Dec. 14, 1943	I	WOLF
Jul. 25, 1942	I	HEARTH	Dec. 27, 1943	I	HEARTH
Aug. 7, 1942	I	OWL	Jan. 9, 1944	I	OWL
Aug. 20, 1942	I	THE RIVER	Jan. 22, 1944	I	THE RIVER
Sept. 2, 1942	I	WHIRLWIND	Feb. 4, 1944	I	WHIRLWIND
Sept. 15, 1942	I	EAGLE	Feb. 17, 1944	I	EAGLE
Sept. 28, 1942	I	RABBIT	Mar. 1, 1944	I	RABBIT
Oct. 11, 1942	I	TURTLE	Mar. 14, 1944	I	TURTLE
Oct. 24, 1942	I	PANTHER	Mar. 27, 1944	I	PANTHER
Nov. 6, 1942	I	DEER	Apr. 9, 1944	I	DEER
Nov. 19, 1942	I	FLOWER	Apr. 22, 1944	I	FLOWER

May 5, 1944	I	REED	Oct. 7, 1945	I	REED
May 18, 1944	I	TWINS	Oct. 20, 1945	I	TWINS
May 31, 1944	I	REDBIRD	Nov. 2, 1945	I	REDBIRD
Jun. 13, 1944	I	RATTLESNAKE TOOTH	Nov. 15, 1945	I	RATTLESNAKE TOOTH
Jun. 26, 1944	I	SERPENT	Nov. 28, 1945	I	SERPENT
Jul. 9, 1944	I	FLINT	Dec. 11, 1945	I	FLINT
Jul. 22, 1944	I	RACCOON	Dec. 24, 1945	I	RACCOON
Aug. 4, 1944	I	DRAGON	Jan. 6, 1946	I	DRAGON
Aug. 17, 1944	I	HERON	Jan. 19, 1946	I	HERON
Aug. 30, 1944	I	WOLF	Feb. 1, 1946	I	WOLF
Sept. 12, 1944	I	HEARTH	Feb. 14, 1946	I	HEARTH
Sept. 25, 1944	I	OWL	Feb. 27, 1946	I	OWL
Oct. 8, 1944	I	THE RIVER	Mar. 12, 1946	I	THE RIVER
Oct. 21, 1944	I	WHIRLWIND	Mar. 25, 1946	I	WHIRLWIND
Nov. 3, 1944	I	EAGLE	Apr. 7, 1946	I	EAGLE
Nov. 16, 1944	I	RABBIT	Apr. 20, 1946	I	RABBIT
Nov. 29, 1944	I	TURTLE	May 3, 1946	I	TURTLE
Dec. 12, 1944	I	PANTHER	May 16, 1946	I	PANTHER
Dec. 25, 1944	I	DEER	May 29, 1946	I	DEER
Jan. 7, 1945	I	FLOWER	Jun. 11, 1946	I	FLOWER
Jan. 20, 1945	I	REED	Jun. 24, 1946	I	REED
Feb. 2, 1945	I	TWINS	Jul. 7, 1946	I	TWINS
Feb. 15, 1945	I	REDBIRD	Jul. 20, 1946	I	REDBIRD
Feb. 28, 1945	I	RATTLESNAKE TOOTH	Aug. 2, 1946	I	RATTLESNAKE TOOTH
Mar. 13, 1945	I	SERPENT	Aug. 15, 1946	I	SERPENT
Mar. 26, 1945	I	FLINT	Aug. 28, 1946	I	FLINT
Apr. 8, 1945	I	RACCOON	Sept. 10, 1946	I	RACCOON
Apr. 21, 1945	I	DRAGON	Sept. 23, 1946	I	DRAGON
May 4, 1945	I	HERON	Oct. 6, 1946	I	HERON
May 17, 1945	I	WOLF	Oct. 19, 1946	I	WOLF
May 30, 1945	I	HEARTH	Nov. 1, 1946	I	HEARTH
Jun. 12, 1945	I	OWL	Nov. 14, 1946	I	OWL
Jun. 25, 1945	I	THE RIVER	Nov. 27, 1946	I	THE RIVER
Jul. 8, 1945	I	WHIRLWIND	Dec. 10, 1946	I	WHIRLWIND
Jul. 21, 1945	I	EAGLE	Dec. 23, 1946	I	EAGLE
Aug. 3, 1945	I	RABBIT	Jan. 5, 1947	I	RABBIT
Aug. 16, 1945	I	TURTLE	Jan. 18, 1947	I	TURTLE
Aug. 29, 1945	I	PANTHER	Jan. 31, 1947	I	PANTHER
Sept. 11, 1945	I	DEER	Feb. 13, 1947	I	DEER
Sept. 24, 1945	I	FLOWER	Feb. 26, 1947	I	FLOWER

Mar. 11, 1947	I	REED	Aug. 12, 1948	I	REED
Mar. 24, 1947	I	TWINS	Aug. 25, 1948	I	TWINS
Apr. 6, 1947	I	REDBIRD	Sept. 7, 1948	I	REDBIRD
Apr. 19, 1947	I	RATTLESNAKE TOOTH	Sept. 20, 1948	I	RATTLESNAKE TOOTH
May 2, 1947	I	SERPENT	Oct. 3, 1948	I	SERPENT
May 15, 1947	I	FLINT	Oct. 16, 1948	I	FLINT
May 28, 1947	I	RACCOON	Oct. 29, 1948	I	RACCOON
Jun. 10, 1947	I	DRAGON	Nov. 11, 1948	I	DRAGON
Jun. 23, 1947	I	HERON	Nov. 24, 1948	I	HERON
Jul. 6, 1947	I	WOLF	Dec. 7, 1948	I	WOLF
Jul. 19, 1947	I	HEARTH	Dec. 20, 1948	I	HEARTH
Aug. 1, 1947	I	OWL	Jan. 2, 1949	I	OWL
Aug. 14, 1947	I	THE RIVER	Jan. 15, 1949	I	THE RIVER
Aug. 27, 1947	I	WHIRLWIND	Jan. 28, 1949	I	WHIRLWIND
Sept. 9, 1947	I	EAGLE	Feb. 10, 1949	I	EAGLE
Sept. 22, 1947	I	RABBIT	Feb. 23, 1949	I	RABBIT
Oct. 5, 1947	I	TURTLE	Mar. 8, 1949	I	TURTLE
Oct. 18, 1947	I	PANTHER	Mar. 21, 1949	I	PANTHER
Oct. 31, 1947	I	DEER	Apr. 3, 1949	I	DEER
Nov. 13, 1947	I	FLOWER	Apr. 16, 1949	I	FLOWER
Nov. 26, 1947	I	REED	Apr. 29, 1949	I	REED
Dec. 9, 1947	I	TWINS	May 12, 1949	I	TWINS
Dec. 22, 1947	I	REDBIRD	May 25, 1949	I	REDBIRD
Jan. 4, 1948	I	RATTLESNAKE TOOTH	Jun. 7, 1949	I	RATTLESNAKE TOOTH
Jan. 17, 1948	I	SERPENT	Jun. 20, 1949	I	SERPENT
Jan. 30, 1948	I	FLINT	Jul. 3, 1949	I	FLINT
Feb. 12, 1948	I	RACCOON	Jul. 16, 1949	I	RACCOON
Feb. 25, 1948	I	DRAGON	Jul. 29, 1949	I	DRAGON
Mar. 9, 1948	I	HERON	Aug. 11, 1949	I	HERON
Mar. 22, 1948	I	WOLF	Aug. 24, 1949	I	WOLF
Apr. 4, 1948	I	HEARTH	Sept. 6, 1949	I	HEARTH
Apr. 17, 1948	I	OWL	Sept. 19, 1949	I	OWL
Apr. 30, 1948	I	THE RIVER	Oct. 2, 1949	I	THE RIVER
May 13, 1948	I	WHIRLWIND	Oct. 15, 1949	I	WHIRLWIND
May 26, 1948	I	EAGLE	Oct. 28, 1949	I	EAGLE
Jun. 8, 1948	I	RABBIT	Nov. 10, 1949	I	RABBIT
Jun. 21, 1948	I	TURTLE	Nov. 23, 1949	I	TURTLE
Jul. 4, 1948	I	PANTHER	Dec. 6, 1949	I	PANTHER
Jul. 17, 1948	I	DEER	Dec. 19, 1949	I	DEER
Jul. 30, 1948	I	FLOWER	Jan. 1, 1950	I	FLOWER

Jan. 14, 1950	I	REED	Jun. 18, 1951	I	REED
Jan. 27, 1950	I	TWINS	Jul. 1, 1951	I	TWINS
Feb. 9, 1950	I	REDBIRD	Jul. 14, 1951	I	REDBIRD
Feb. 22, 1950	I	RATTLESNAKE TOOTH	Jul. 27, 1951	I	RATTLESNAKE TOOTH
Mar. 7, 1950	I	SERPENT	Aug. 9, 1951	I	SERPENT
Mar. 20, 1950	I	FLINT	Aug. 22, 1951	I	FLINT
Apr. 2, 1950	I	RACCOON	Sept. 4, 1951	I	RACCOON
Apr. 15, 1950	I	DRAGON	Sept. 17, 1951	I	DRAGON
Apr. 28, 1950	I	HERON	Sept. 30, 1951	I	HERON
May 11, 1950	I	WOLF	Oct. 13, 1951	I	WOLF
May 24, 1950	I	HEARTH	Oct. 26, 1951	I	HEARTH
Jun. 6, 1950	I	OWL	Nov. 8, 1951	I	OWL
Jun. 19, 1950	I	THE RIVER	Nov. 21, 1951	I	THE RIVER
Jul. 2, 1950	I	WHIRLWIND	Dec. 4, 1951	I	WHIRLWIND
Jul. 15, 1950	I	EAGLE	Dec. 17, 1951	I	EAGLE
Jul. 28, 1950	I	RABBIT	Dec. 30, 1951	I	RABBIT
Aug. 10, 1950	I	TURTLE	Jan. 12, 1952	I	TURTLE
Aug. 23, 1950	I	PANTHER	Jan. 25, 1952	I	PANTHER
Sept. 5, 1950	I	DEER	Feb. 7, 1952	I	DEER
Sept. 18, 1950	I	FLOWER	Feb. 20, 1952	I	FLOWER
Oct. 1, 1950	I	REED	Mar. 4, 1952	I	REED
Oct. 14, 1950	I	TWINS	Mar. 17, 1952	I	TWINS
Oct. 27, 1950	I	REDBIRD	Mar. 30, 1952	I	REDBIRD
Nov. 9, 1950	I	RATTLESNAKE TOOTH	Apr. 12, 1952	I	RATTLESNAKE TOOTH
Nov. 22, 1950	I	SERPENT	Apr. 25, 1952	I	SERPENT
Dec. 5, 1950	I	FLINT	May 8, 1952	I	FLINT
Dec. 18, 1950	I	RACCOON	May 21, 1952	I	RACCOON
Dec. 31, 1950	I	DRAGON	Jun. 3, 1952	I	DRAGON
Jan. 13, 1951	I	HERON	Jun. 16, 1952	I	HERON
Jan. 26, 1951	I	WOLF	Jun. 29, 1952	I	WOLF
Feb. 8, 1951	I	HEARTH	Jul. 12, 1952	I	HEARTH
Feb. 21, 1951	I	OWL	Jul. 25, 1952	I	OWL
Mar. 6, 1951	I	THE RIVER	Aug. 7, 1952	I	THE RIVER
Mar. 19, 1951	I	WHIRLWIND	Aug. 20, 1952	I	WHIRLWIND
Apr. 1, 1951	I	EAGLE	Sept. 2, 1952	I	EAGLE
Apr. 14, 1951	I	RABBIT	Sept. 15, 1952	I	RABBIT
Apr. 27, 1951	I	TURTLE	Sept. 28, 1952	I	TURTLE
May 10, 1951	I	PANTHER	Oct. 11, 1952	I	PANTHER
May 23, 1951	I	DEER	Oct. 24, 1952	I	DEER
Jun. 5, 1951	I	FLOWER	Nov. 6, 1952	I	FLOWER

Nov. 19, 1952	I	REED	Apr. 23, 1954	I	REED
Dec. 2, 1952	I	TWINS	May 6, 1954	I	TWINS
Dec. 15, 1952	I	REDBIRD	May 19, 1954	I	REDBIRD
Dec. 28, 1952	I	RATTLESNAKE TOOTH	Jun. 1, 1954	I	RATTLESNAKE TOOTH
Jan. 10, 1953	I	SERPENT	Jun. 14, 1954	I	SERPENT
Jan. 23, 1953	I	FLINT	Jun. 27, 1954	I	FLINT
Feb. 5, 1953	I	RACCOON	Jul. 10, 1954	I	RACCOON
Feb. 18, 1953	I	DRAGON	Jul. 23, 1954	I	DRAGON
Mar. 3, 1953	I	HERON	Aug. 5, 1954	I	HERON
Mar. 16, 1953	I	WOLF	Aug. 18, 1954	I	WOLF
Mar. 29, 1953	I	HEARTH	Aug. 31, 1954	I	HEARTH
Apr. 11, 1953	I	OWL	Sept. 13, 1954	I	OWL
Apr. 24, 1953	I	THE RIVER	Sept. 26, 1954	I	THE RIVER
May 7, 1953	I	WHIRLWIND	Oct. 9, 1954	I	WHIRLWIND
May 20, 1953	I	EAGLE	Oct. 22, 1954	I	EAGLE
Jun. 2, 1953	I	RABBIT	Nov. 4, 1954	I	RABBIT
Jun. 15, 1953	I	TURTLE	Nov. 17, 1954	I	TURTLE
Jun. 28, 1953	I	PANTHER	Nov. 30, 1954	I	PANTHER
Jul. 11, 1953	I	DEER	Dec. 13, 1954	I	DEER
Jul. 24, 1953	I	FLOWER	Dec. 26, 1954	I	FLOWER
Aug. 6, 1953	I	REED	Jan. 8, 1955	I	REED
Aug. 19, 1953	I	TWINS	Jan. 21, 1955	I	TWINS
Sept. 1, 1953	I	REDBIRD	Feb. 3, 1955	I	REDBIRD
Sept. 14, 1953	I	RATTLESNAKE TOOTH	Feb. 16, 1955	I	RATTLESNAKE TOOTH
Sept. 27, 1953	I	SERPENT	Mar. 1, 1955	I	SERPENT
Oct. 10, 1953	I	FLINT	Mar. 14, 1955	I	FLINT
Oct. 23, 1953	I	RACCOON	Mar. 27, 1955	I	RACCOON
Nov. 5, 1953	I	DRAGON	Apr. 9, 1955	I	DRAGON
Nov. 18, 1953	I	HERON	Apr. 22, 1955	I	HERON
Dec. 1, 1953	I	WOLF	May 5, 1955	I	WOLF
Dec. 14, 1953	I	HEARTH	May 18, 1955	I	HEARTH
Dec. 27, 1953	I	OWL	May 31, 1955	I	OWL
Jan. 9, 1954	I	THE RIVER	Jun. 13, 1955	I	THE RIVER
Jan. 22, 1954	I	WHIRLWIND	Jun. 26, 1955	I	WHIRLWIND
Feb. 4, 1954	I	EAGLE	Jul. 9, 1955	I	EAGLE
Feb. 17, 1954	I	RABBIT	Jul. 22, 1955	I	RABBIT
Mar. 2, 1954	I	TURTLE	Aug. 4, 1955	I	TURTLE
Mar. 15, 1954	I	PANTHER	Aug. 17, 1955	I	PANTHER
Mar. 28, 1954	I	DEER	Aug. 30, 1955	I	DEER
Apr. 10, 1954	I	FLOWER	Sept. 12, 1955	I	FLOWER

Sept. 25, 1955	REED	Feb. 26, 1957	REED
Oct. 8, 1955	TWINS	Mar. 11, 1957	TWINS
Oct. 21, 1955	REDBIRD	Mar. 24, 1957	REDBIRD
Nov. 3, 1955	RATTLESNAKE TOOTH	Apr. 6, 1957	RATTLESNAKE TOOTH
Nov. 16, 1955	SERPENT	Apr. 19, 1957	SERPENT
Nov. 29, 1955	FLINT	May 2, 1957	FLINT
Dec. 12, 1955	RACCOON	May 15, 1957	RACCOON
Dec. 25, 1955	DRAGON	May 28, 1957	DRAGON
Jan. 7, 1956	HERON	Jun. 10, 1957	HERON
Jan. 20, 1956	WOLF	Jun. 23, 1957	WOLF
Feb. 2, 1956	HEARTH	Jul. 6, 1957	HEARTH
Feb. 15, 1956	OWL	Jul. 19, 1957	OWL
Feb. 28, 1956	THE RIVER	Aug. 1, 1957	THE RIVER
Mar. 12, 1956	WHIRLWIND	Aug. 14, 1957	WHIRLWIND
Mar. 25, 1956	EAGLE	Aug. 27, 1957	EAGLE
Apr. 7, 1956	RABBIT	Sept. 9, 1957	RABBIT
Apr. 20, 1956	TURTLE	Sept. 22, 1957	TURTLE
May 3, 1956	PANTHER	Oct. 5, 1957	PANTHER
May 16, 1956	DEER	Oct. 18, 1957	DEER
May 29, 1956	FLOWER	Oct. 31, 1957	FLOWER
Jun. 11, 1956	REED	Nov. 13, 1957	REED
Jun. 24, 1956	TWINS	Nov. 26, 1957	TWINS
Jul. 7, 1956	REDBIRD	Dec. 9, 1957	REDBIRD
Jul. 20, 1956	RATTLESNAKE TOOTH	Dec. 22, 1957	RATTLESNAKE TOOTH
Aug. 2, 1956	SERPENT	Jan. 4, 1958	SERPENT
Aug. 15, 1956	FLINT	Jan. 17, 1958	FLINT
Aug. 28, 1956	RACCOON	Jan. 30, 1958	RACCOON
Sept. 10, 1956	DRAGON	Feb. 12, 1958	DRAGON
Sept. 23, 1956	HERON	Feb. 25, 1958	HERON
Oct. 6, 1956	WOLF	Mar. 10, 1958	WOLF
Oct. 19, 1956	HEARTH	Mar. 23, 1958	HEARTH
Nov. 1, 1956	OWL	Apr. 5, 1958	OWL
Nov. 14, 1956	THE RIVER	Apr. 18, 1958	THE RIVER
Nov. 27, 1956	WHIRLWIND	May 1, 1958	WHIRLWIND
Dec. 10, 1956	EAGLE	May 14, 1958	EAGLE
Dec. 23, 1956	RABBIT	May 27, 1958	RABBIT
Jan. 5, 1957	TURTLE	Jun. 9, 1958	TURTLE
Jan. 18, 1957	PANTHER	Jun. 22, 1958	PANTHER
Jan. 31, 1957	DEER	Jul. 5, 1958	DEER
Feb. 13, 1957	FLOWER	Jul. 18, 1958	FLOWER

Jul. 31, 1958	I	REED
Aug. 13, 1958	I	TWINS
Aug. 26, 1958	I	REDBIRD
Sept. 8, 1958	I	RATTLESNAKE TOOTH
Sept. 21, 1958	I	SERPENT
Oct. 4, 1958	I	FLINT
Oct. 17, 1958	I	RACCOON
Oct. 30, 1958	I	DRAGON
Nov. 12, 1958	I	HERON
Nov. 25, 1958	I	WOLF
Dec. 8, 1958	I	HEARTH
Dec. 21, 1958	I	OWL
Jan. 3, 1959	I	THE RIVER
Jan. 16, 1959	I	WHIRLWIND
Jan. 29, 1959	I	EAGLE
Feb. 11, 1959	I	RABBIT
Feb. 24, 1959	I	TURTLE
Mar. 9, 1959	I	PANTHER
Mar. 22, 1959	I	DEER
Apr. 4, 1959	I	FLOWER
Apr. 17, 1959	I	REED
Apr. 30, 1959	I	TWINS
May 13, 1959	I	REDBIRD
May 26, 1959	I	RATTLESNAKE TOOTH
Jun. 8, 1959	I	SERPENT
Jun. 21, 1959	I	FLINT
Jul. 4, 1959	I	RACCOON
Jul. 17, 1959	I	DRAGON
Jul. 30, 1959	I	HERON
Aug. 12, 1959	I	WOLF
Aug. 25, 1959	I	HEARTH
Sept. 7, 1959	I	OWL
Sept. 20, 1959	I	THE RIVER
Oct. 3, 1959	I	WHIRLWIND
Oct. 16, 1959	I	EAGLE
Oct. 29, 1959	I	RABBIT
Nov. 11, 1959	I	TURTLE
Nov. 24, 1959	I	PANTHER
Dec. 7, 1959	I	DEER
Dec. 20, 1959	I	FLOWER

Jan. 2, 1960	I	REED
Jan. 15, 1960	I	TWINS
Jan. 28, 1960	I	REDBIRD
Feb. 10, 1960	I	RATTLESNAKE TOOTH
Feb. 23, 1960	I	SERPENT
Mar. 7, 1960	I	FLINT
Mar. 20, 1960	I	RACCOON
Apr. 2, 1960	I	DRAGON
Apr. 15, 1960	I	HERON
Apr. 28, 1960	I	WOLF
May 11, 1960	I	HEARTH
May 24, 1960	I	OWL
Jun. 6, 1960	I	THE RIVER
Jun. 19, 1960	I	WHIRLWIND
Jul. 2, 1960	I	EAGLE
Jul. 15, 1960	I	RABBIT
Jul. 28, 1960	I	TURTLE
Aug. 10, 1960	I	PANTHER
Aug. 23, 1960	I	DEER
Sept. 5, 1960	I	FLOWER
Sept. 18, 1960	I	REED
Oct. 1, 1960	I	TWINS
Oct. 14, 1960	I	REDBIRD
Oct. 27, 1960	I	RATTLESNAKE TOOTH
Nov. 9, 1960	I	SERPENT
Nov. 22, 1960	I	FLINT
Dec. 5, 1960	I	RACCOON
Dec. 18, 1960	I	DRAGON
Dec. 31, 1960	I	HERON
Jan. 13, 1961	I	WOLF
Jan. 26, 1961	I	HEARTH
Feb. 8, 1961	I	OWL
Feb. 21, 1961	I	THE RIVER
Mar. 6, 1961	I	WHIRLWIND
Mar. 19, 1961	I	EAGLE
Apr. 1, 1961	I	RABBIT
Apr. 14, 1961	I	TURTLE
Apr. 27, 1961	I	PANTHER
May 10, 1961	I	DEER
May 23, 1961	I	FLOWER

Jun. 5, 1961	I	REED	Nov. 7, 1962	I	REED
Jun. 18, 1961	I	TWINS	Nov. 20, 1962	I	TWINS
Jul. 1, 1961	I	REDBIRD	Dec. 3, 1962	I	REDBIRD
Jul. 14, 1961	I	RATTLESNAKE TOOTH	Dec. 16, 1962	I	RATTLESNAKE TOOTH
Jul. 27, 1961	I	SERPENT	Dec. 29, 1962	I	SERPENT
Aug. 9, 1961	I	FLINT	Jan. 11, 1963	I	FLINT
Aug. 22, 1961	I	RACCOON	Jan. 24, 1963	I	RACCOON
Sept. 4, 1961	I	DRAGON	Feb. 6, 1963	I	DRAGON
Sept. 17, 1961	I	HERON	Feb. 19, 1963	I	HERON
Sept. 30, 1961	I	WOLF	Mar. 4, 1963	I	WOLF
Oct. 13, 1961	I	HEARTH	Mar. 17, 1963	I	HEARTH
Oct. 26, 1961	I	OWL	Mar. 30, 1963	I	OWL
Nov. 8, 1961	I	THE RIVER	Apr. 12, 1963	I	THE RIVER
Nov. 21, 1961	I	WHIRLWIND	Apr. 25, 1963	I	WHIRLWIND
Dec. 4, 1961	I	EAGLE	May 8, 1963	I	EAGLE
Dec. 17, 1961	I	RABBIT	May 21, 1963	I	RABBIT
Dec. 30, 1961	I	TURTLE	Jun. 3, 1963	I	TURTLE
Jan. 12, 1962	I	PANTHER	Jun. 16, 1963	I	PANTHER
Jan. 25, 1962	I	DEER	Jun. 29, 1963	I	DEER
Feb. 7, 1962	I	FLOWER	Jul. 12, 1963	I	FLOWER
Feb. 20, 1962	I	REED	Jul. 25, 1963	I	REED
Mar. 5, 1962	I	TWINS	Aug. 7, 1963	I	TWINS
Mar. 18, 1962	I	REDBIRD	Aug. 20, 1963	I	REDBIRD
Mar. 31, 1962	I	RATTLESNAKE TOOTH	Sept. 2, 1963	I	RATTLESNAKE TOOTH
Apr. 13, 1962	I	SERPENT	Sept. 15, 1963	I	SERPENT
Apr. 26, 1962	I	FLINT	Sept. 28, 1963	I	FLINT
May 9, 1962	I	RACCOON	Oct. 11, 1963	I	RACCOON
May 22, 1962	I	DRAGON	Oct. 24, 1963	I	DRAGON
Jun. 4, 1962	I	HERON	Nov. 6, 1963	I	HERON
Jun. 17, 1962	I	WOLF	Nov. 19, 1963	I	WOLF
Jun. 30, 1962	I	HEARTH	Dec. 2, 1963	I	HEARTH
Jul. 13, 1962	I	OWL	Dec. 15, 1963	I	OWL
Jul. 26, 1962	I	THE RIVER	Dec. 28, 1963	I	THE RIVER
Aug. 8, 1962	I	WHIRLWIND	Jan. 10, 1964	I	WHIRLWIND
Aug. 21, 1962	I	EAGLE	Jan. 23, 1964	I	EAGLE
Sept. 3, 1962	I	RABBIT	Feb. 5, 1964	I	RABBIT
Sept. 16, 1962	I	TURTLE	Feb. 18, 1964	I	TURTLE
Sept. 29, 1962	I	PANTHER	Mar. 2, 1964	I	PANTHER
Oct. 12, 1962	I	DEER	Mar. 15, 1964	I	DEER
Oct. 25, 1962	I	FLOWER	Mar. 28, 1964	I	FLOWER

Apr. 10, 1964	I	REED	Sept. 12, 1965	I	REED
Apr. 23, 1964	I	TWINS	Sept. 25, 1965	I	TWINS
May 6, 1964	I	REDBIRD	Oct. 8, 1965	I	REDBIRD
May 19, 1964	I	RATTLESNAKE TOOTH	Oct. 21, 1965	I	RATTLESNAKE TOOTH
Jun. 1, 1964	I	SERPENT	Nov. 3, 1965	I	SERPENT
Jun. 14, 1964	I	FLINT	Nov. 16, 1965	I	FLINT
Jun. 27, 1964	I	RACCOON	Nov. 29, 1965	I	RACCOON
Jul. 10, 1964	I	DRAGON	Dec. 12, 1965	I	DRAGON
Jul. 23, 1964	I	HERON	Dec. 25, 1965	I	HERON
Aug. 5, 1964	I	WOLF	Jan. 7, 1966	I	WOLF
Aug. 18, 1964	I	HEARTH	Jan. 20, 1966	I	HEARTH
Aug. 31, 1964	I	OWL	Feb. 2, 1966	I	OWL
Sept. 13, 1964	I	THE RIVER	Feb. 15, 1966	I	THE RIVER
Sept. 26, 1964	I	WHIRLWIND	Feb. 28, 1966	I	WHIRLWIND
Oct. 9, 1964	I	EAGLE	Mar. 13, 1966	I	EAGLE
Oct. 22, 1964	I	RABBIT	Mar. 26, 1966	I	RABBIT
Nov. 4, 1964	I	TURTLE	Apr. 8, 1966	I	TURTLE
Nov. 17, 1964	I	PANTHER	Apr. 21, 1966	I	PANTHER
Nov. 30, 1964	I	DEER	May 4, 1966	I	DEER
Dec. 13, 1964	I	FLOWER	May 17, 1966	I	FLOWER
Dec. 26, 1964	I	REED	May 30, 1966	I	REED
Jan. 8, 1965	I	TWINS	Jun. 12, 1966	I	TWINS
Jan. 21, 1965	I	REDBIRD	Jun. 25, 1966	I	REDBIRD
Feb. 3, 1965	I	RATTLESNAKE TOOTH	Jul. 8, 1966	I	RATTLESNAKE TOOTH
Feb. 16, 1965	I	SERPENT	Jul. 21, 1966	I	SERPENT
Mar. 1, 1965	I	FLINT	Aug. 3, 1966	I	FLINT
Mar. 14, 1965	I	RACCOON	Aug. 16, 1966	I	RACCOON
Mar. 27, 1965	I	DRAGON	Aug. 29, 1966	I	DRAGON
Apr. 9, 1965	I	HERON	Sept. 11, 1966	I	HERON
Apr. 22, 1965	I	WOLF	Sept. 24, 1966	I	WOLF
May 5, 1965	I	HEARTH	Oct. 7, 1966	I	HEARTH
May 18, 1965	I	OWL	Oct. 20, 1966	I	OWL
May 31, 1965	I	THE RIVER	Nov. 2, 1966	I	THE RIVER
Jun. 13, 1965	I	WHIRLWIND	Nov. 15, 1966	I	WHIRLWIND
Jun. 26, 1965	I	EAGLE	Nov. 28, 1966	I	EAGLE
Jul. 9, 1965	I	RABBIT	Dec. 11, 1966	I	RABBIT
Jul. 22, 1965	I	TURTLE	Dec. 24, 1966	I	TURTLE
Aug. 4, 1965	I	PANTHER	Jan. 6, 1967	I	PANTHER
Aug. 17, 1965	I	DEER	Jan. 19, 1967	I	DEER
Aug. 30, 1965	I	FLOWER	Feb. 1, 1967	I	FLOWER

Feb. 14, 1967	REED
Feb. 27, 1967	TWINS
Mar. 12, 1967	REDBIRD
Mar. 25, 1967	RATTLESNAKE TOOTH
Apr. 7, 1967	SERPENT
Apr. 20, 1967	FLINT
May 3, 1967	RACCOON
May 16, 1967	DRAGON
May 29, 1967	HERON
Jun. 11, 1967	WOLF
Jun. 24, 1967	HEARTH
Jul. 7, 1967	OWL
Jul. 20, 1967	THE RIVER
Aug. 2, 1967	WHIRLWIND
Aug. 15, 1967	EAGLE
Aug. 28, 1967	RABBIT
Sept. 10, 1967	TURTLE
Sept. 23, 1967	PANTHER
Oct. 6, 1967	DEER
Oct. 19, 1967	FLOWER
Nov. 1, 1967	REED
Nov. 14, 1967	TWINS
Nov. 27, 1967	REDBIRD
Dec. 10, 1967	RATTLESNAKE TOOTH
Dec. 23, 1967	SERPENT
Jan. 5, 1968	FLINT
Jan. 18, 1968	RACCOON
Jan. 31, 1968	DRAGON
Feb. 13, 1968	HERON
Feb. 26, 1968	WOLF
Mar. 10, 1968	HEARTH
Mar. 23, 1968	OWL
Apr. 5, 1968	THE RIVER
Apr. 18, 1968	WHIRLWIND
May 1, 1968	EAGLE
May 14, 1968	RABBIT
May 27, 1968	TURTLE
Jun. 9, 1968	PANTHER
Jun. 22, 1968	DEER
Jul. 5, 1968	FLOWER

Jul. 18, 1968	REED
Jul. 31, 1968	TWINS
Aug. 13, 1968	REDBIRD
Aug. 26, 1968	RATTLESNAKE TOOTH
Sept. 8, 1968	SERPENT
Sept. 21, 1968	FLINT
Oct. 4, 1968	RACCOON
Oct. 17, 1968	DRAGON
Oct. 30, 1968	HERON
Nov. 12, 1968	WOLF
Nov. 25, 1968	HEARTH
Dec. 8, 1968	OWL
Dec. 21, 1968	THE RIVER
Jan. 3, 1969	WHIRLWIND
Jan. 16, 1969	EAGLE
Jan. 29, 1969	RABBIT
Feb. 11, 1969	TURTLE
Feb. 24, 1969	PANTHER
Mar. 9, 1969	DEER
Mar. 22, 1969	FLOWER
Apr. 4, 1969	REED
Apr. 17, 1969	TWINS
Apr. 30, 1969	REDBIRD
May 13, 1969	RATTLESNAKE TOOTH
May 26, 1969	SERPENT
Jun. 8, 1969	FLINT
Jun. 21, 1969	RACCOON
Jul. 4, 1969	DRAGON
Jul. 17, 1969	HERON
Jul. 30, 1969	WOLF
Aug. 12, 1969	HEARTH
Aug. 25, 1969	OWL
Sept. 7, 1969	THE RIVER
Sept. 20, 1969	WHIRLWIND
Oct. 3, 1969	EAGLE
Oct. 16, 1969	RABBIT
Oct. 29, 1969	TURTLE
Nov. 11, 1969	PANTHER
Nov. 24, 1969	DEER
Dec. 7, 1969	FLOWER

Dec. 20, 1969	I	REED	May 24, 1971	I	REED
Jan. 2, 1970	I	TWINS	Jun. 6, 1971	I	TWINS
Jan. 15, 1970	I	REDBIRD	Jun. 19, 1971	I	REDBIRD
Jan. 28, 1970	I	RATTLESNAKE TOOTH	Jul. 2, 1971	I	RATTLESNAKE TOOTH
Feb. 10, 1970	I	SERPENT	Jul. 15, 1971	I	SERPENT
Feb. 23, 1970	I	FLINT	Jul. 28, 1971	I	FLINT
Mar. 8, 1970	I	RACCOON	Aug. 10, 1971	I	RACCOON
Mar. 21, 1970	I	DRAGON	Aug. 23, 1971	I	DRAGON
Apr. 3, 1970	I	HERON	Sept. 5, 1971	I	HERON
Apr. 16, 1970	I	WOLF	Sept. 18, 1971	I	WOLF
Apr. 29, 1970	I	HEARTH	Oct. 1, 1971	I	HEARTH
May 12, 1970	I	OWL	Oct. 14, 1971	I	OWL
May 25, 1970	I	THE RIVER	Oct. 27, 1971	I	THE RIVER
Jun. 7, 1970	I	WHIRLWIND	Nov. 9, 1971	I	WHIRLWIND
Jun. 20, 1970	I	EAGLE	Nov. 22, 1971	I	EAGLE
Jul. 3, 1970	I	RABBIT	Dec. 5, 1971	I	RABBIT
Jul. 16, 1970	I	TURTLE	Dec. 18, 1971	I	TURTLE
Jul. 29, 1970	I	PANTHER	Dec. 31, 1971	I	PANTHER
Aug. 11, 1970	I	DEER	Jan. 13, 1972	I	DEER
Aug. 24, 1970	I	FLOWER	Jan. 26, 1972	I	FLOWER
Sept. 6, 1970	I	REED	Feb. 8, 1972	I	REED
Sept. 19, 1970	I	TWINS	Feb. 21, 1972	I	TWINS
Oct. 2, 1970	I	REDBIRD	Mar. 5, 1972	I	REDBIRD
Oct. 15, 1970	I	RATTLESNAKE TOOTH	Mar. 18, 1972	I	RATTLESNAKE TOOTH
Oct. 28, 1970	I	SERPENT	Mar. 31, 1972	I	SERPENT
Nov. 10, 1970	I	FLINT	Apr. 13, 1972	I	FLINT
Nov. 23, 1970	I	RACCOON	Apr. 26, 1972	I	RACCOON
Dec. 6, 1970	I	DRAGON	May 9, 1972	I	DRAGON
Dec. 19, 1970	I	HERON	May 22, 1972	I	HERON
Jan. 1, 1971	I	WOLF	Jun. 4, 1972	I	WOLF
Jan. 14, 1971	I	HEARTH	Jun. 17, 1972	I	HEARTH
Jan. 27, 1971	I	OWL	Jun. 30, 1972	I	OWL
Feb. 9, 1971	I	THE RIVER	Jul. 13, 1972	I	THE RIVER
Feb. 22, 1971	I	WHIRLWIND	Jul. 26, 1972	I	WHIRLWIND
Mar. 7, 1971	I	EAGLE	Aug. 8, 1972	I	EAGLE
Mar. 20, 1971	I	RABBIT	Aug. 21, 1972	I	RABBIT
Apr. 2, 1971	I	TURTLE	Sept. 3, 1972	I	TURTLE
Apr. 15, 1971	I	PANTHER	Sept. 16, 1972	I	PANTHER
Apr. 28, 1971	I	DEER	Sept. 29, 1972	I	DEER
May 11, 1971	I	FLOWER	Oct. 12, 1972	I	FLOWER

Oct. 25, 1972	I	REED	Mar. 29, 1974	I	REED
Nov. 7, 1972	I	TWINS	Apr. 11, 1974	I	TWINS
Nov. 20, 1972	I	REDBIRD	Apr. 24, 1974	I	REDBIRD
Dec. 3, 1972	I	RATTLESNAKE TOOTH	May 7, 1974	I	RATTLESNAKE TOOTH
Dec. 16, 1972	I	SERPENT	May 20, 1974	I	SERPENT
Dec. 29, 1972	I	FLINT	Jun. 2, 1974	I	FLINT
Jan. 11, 1973	I	RACCOON	Jun. 15, 1974	I	RACCOON
Jan. 24, 1973	I	DRAGON	Jun. 28, 1974	I	DRAGON
Feb. 6, 1973	I	HERON	Jul. 11, 1974	I	HERON
Feb. 19, 1973	I	WOLF	Jul. 24, 1974	I	WOLF
Mar. 4, 1973	I	HEARTH	Aug. 6, 1974	I	HEARTH
Mar. 17, 1973	I	OWL	Aug. 19, 1974	I	OWL
Mar. 30, 1973	I	THE RIVER	Sept. 1, 1974	I	THE RIVER
Apr. 12, 1973	I	WHIRLWIND	Sept. 14, 1974	I	WHIRLWIND
Apr. 25, 1973	I	EAGLE	Sept. 27, 1974	I	EAGLE
May 8, 1973	I	RABBIT	Oct. 10, 1974	I	RABBIT
May 21, 1973	I	TURTLE	Oct. 23, 1974	I	TURTLE
Jun. 3, 1973	I	PANTHER	Nov. 5, 1974	I	PANTHER
Jun. 16, 1973	I	DEER	Nov. 18, 1974	I	DEER
Jun. 29, 1973	I	FLOWER	Dec. 1, 1974	I	FLOWER
Jul. 12, 1973	I	REED	Dec. 14, 1974	I	REED
Jul. 25, 1973	I	TWINS	Dec. 27, 1974	I	TWINS
Aug. 7, 1973	I	REDBIRD	Jan. 9, 1975	I	REDBIRD
Aug. 20, 1973	I	RATTLESNAKE TOOTH	Jan. 22, 1975	I	RATTLESNAKE TOOTH
Sept. 2, 1973	I	SERPENT	Feb. 4, 1975	I	SERPENT
Sept. 15, 1973	I	FLINT	Feb. 17, 1975	I	FLINT
Sept. 28, 1973	I	RACCOON	Mar. 2, 1975	I	RACCOON
Oct. 11, 1973	I	DRAGON	Mar. 15, 1975	I	DRAGON
Oct. 24, 1973	I	HERON	Mar. 28, 1975	I	HERON
Nov. 6, 1973	I	WOLF	Apr. 10, 1975	I	WOLF
Nov. 19, 1973	I	HEARTH	Apr. 23, 1975	I	HEARTH
Dec. 2, 1973	I	OWL	May 6, 1975	I	OWL
Dec. 15, 1973	I	THE RIVER	May 19, 1975	I	THE RIVER
Dec. 28, 1973	I	WHIRLWIND	Jun. 1, 1975	I	WHIRLWIND
Jan. 10, 1974	I	EAGLE	Jun. 14, 1975	I	EAGLE
Jan. 23, 1974	I	RABBIT	Jun. 27, 1975	I	RABBIT
Feb. 5, 1974	I	TURTLE	Jul. 10, 1975	I	TURTLE
Feb. 18, 1974	I	PANTHER	Jul. 23, 1975	I	PANTHER
Mar. 3, 1974	I	DEER	Aug. 5, 1975	I	DEER
Mar. 16, 1974	I	FLOWER	Aug. 18, 1975	I	FLOWER

Aug. 31, 1975	I	REED	Feb. 1, 1977	I	REED
Sept. 13, 1975	I	TWINS	Feb. 14, 1977	I	TWINS
Sept. 26, 1975	I	REDBIRD	Feb. 27, 1977	I	REDBIRD
Oct. 9, 1975	I	RATTLESNAKE TOOTH	Mar. 12, 1977	I	RATTLESNAKE TOOTH
Oct. 22, 1975	I	SERPENT	Mar. 25, 1977	I	SERPENT
Nov. 4, 1975	I	FLINT	Apr. 7, 1977	I	FLINT
Nov. 17, 1975	I	RACCOON	Apr. 20, 1977	I	RACCOON
Nov. 30, 1975	I	DRAGON	May 3, 1977	I	DRAGON
Dec. 13, 1975	I	HERON	May 16, 1977	I	HERON
Dec. 26, 1975	I	WOLF	May 29, 1977	I	WOLF
Jan. 8, 1976	I	HEARTH	Jun. 11, 1977	I	HEARTH
Jan. 21, 1976	I	OWL	Jun. 24, 1977	I	OWL
Feb. 3, 1976	I	THE RIVER	Jul. 7, 1977	I	THE RIVER
Feb. 16, 1976	I	WHIRLWIND	Jul. 20, 1977	I	WHIRLWIND
Feb. 29, 1976	I	EAGLE	Aug. 2, 1977	I	EAGLE
Mar. 13, 1976	I	RABBIT	Aug. 15, 1977	I	RABBIT
Mar. 26, 1976	I	TURTLE	Aug. 28, 1977	I	TURTLE
Apr. 8, 1976	I	PANTHER	Sept. 10, 1977	I	PANTHER
Apr. 21, 1976	I	DEER	Sept. 23, 1977	I	DEER
May 4, 1976	I	FLOWER	Oct. 6, 1977	I	FLOWER
May 17, 1976	I	REED	Oct. 19, 1977	I	REED
May 30, 1976	I	TWINS	Nov. 1, 1977	I	TWINS
Jun. 12, 1976	I	REDBIRD	Nov. 14, 1977	I	REDBIRD
Jun. 25, 1976	I	RATTLESNAKE TOOTH	Nov. 27, 1977	I	RATTLESNAKE TOOTH
Jul. 8, 1976	I	SERPENT	Dec. 10, 1977	I	SERPENT
Jul. 21, 1976	I	FLINT	Dec. 23, 1977	I	FLINT
Aug. 3, 1976	I	RACCOON	Jan. 5, 1978	I	RACCOON
Aug. 16, 1976	I	DRAGON	Jan. 18, 1978	I	DRAGON
Aug. 29, 1976	I	HERON	Jan. 31, 1978	I	HERON
Sept. 11, 1976	I	WOLF	Feb. 13, 1978	I	WOLF
Sept. 24, 1976	I	HEARTH	Feb. 26, 1978	I	HEARTH
Oct. 7, 1976	I	OWL	Mar. 11, 1978	I	OWL
Oct. 20, 1976	I	THE RIVER	Mar. 24, 1978	I	THE RIVER
Nov. 2, 1976	I	WHIRLWIND	Apr. 6, 1978	I	WHIRLWIND
Nov. 15, 1976	I	EAGLE	Apr. 19, 1978	I	EAGLE
Nov. 28, 1976	I	RABBIT	May 2, 1978	I	RABBIT
Dec. 11, 1976	I	TURTLE	May 15, 1978	I	TURTLE
Dec. 24, 1976	I	PANTHER	May 28, 1978	I	PANTHER
Jan. 6, 1977	I	DEER	Jun. 10, 1978	I	DEER
Jan. 19, 1977	I	FLOWER	Jun. 23, 1978	I	FLOWER

Jul. 6, 1978	REED	Dec. 8, 1979	REED
Jul. 19, 1978	TWINS	Dec. 21, 1979	TWINS
Aug. 1, 1978	REDBIRD	Jan. 3, 1980	REDBIRD
Aug. 14, 1978	RATTLESNAKE TOOTH	Jan. 16, 1980	RATTLESNAKE TOOTH
Aug. 27, 1978	SERPENT	Jan. 29, 1980	SERPENT
Sept. 9, 1978	FLINT	Feb. 11, 1980	FLINT
Sept. 22, 1978	RACCOON	Feb. 24, 1980	RACCOON
Oct. 5, 1978	DRAGON	Mar. 8, 1980	DRAGON
Oct. 18, 1978	HERON	Mar. 21, 1980	HERON
Oct. 31, 1978	WOLF	Apr. 3, 1980	WOLF
Nov. 13, 1978	HEARTH	Apr. 16, 1980	HEARTH
Nov. 26, 1978	OWL	Apr. 29, 1980	OWL
Dec. 9, 1978	THE RIVER	May 12, 1980	THE RIVER
Dec. 22, 1978	WHIRLWIND	May 25, 1980	WHIRLWIND
Jan. 4, 1979	EAGLE	Jun. 7, 1980	EAGLE
Jan. 17, 1979	RABBIT	Jun. 20, 1980	RABBIT
Jan. 30, 1979	TURTLE	Jul. 3, 1980	TURTLE
Feb. 12, 1979	PANTHER	Jul. 16, 1980	PANTHER
Feb. 25, 1979	DEER	Jul. 29, 1980	DEER
Mar. 10, 1979	FLOWER	Aug. 11, 1980	FLOWER
Mar. 23, 1979	REED	Aug. 24, 1980	REED
Apr. 5, 1979	TWINS	Sept. 6, 1980	TWINS
Apr. 18, 1979	REDBIRD	Sept. 19, 1980	REDBIRD
May 1, 1979	RATTLESNAKE TOOTH	Oct. 2, 1980	RATTLESNAKE TOOTH
May 14, 1979	SERPENT	Oct. 15, 1980	SERPENT
May 27, 1979	FLINT	Oct. 28, 1980	FLINT
Jun. 9, 1979	RACCOON	Nov. 10, 1980	RACCOON
Jun. 22, 1979	DRAGON	Nov. 23, 1980	DRAGON
Jul. 5, 1979	HERON	Dec. 6, 1980	HERON
Jul. 18, 1979	WOLF	Dec. 19, 1980	WOLF
Jul. 31, 1979	HEARTH	Jan. 1, 1981	HEARTH
Aug. 13, 1979	OWL	Jan. 14, 1981	OWL
Aug. 26, 1979	THE RIVER	Jan. 27, 1981	THE RIVER
Sept. 8, 1979	WHIRLWIND	Feb. 9, 1981	WHIRLWIND
Sept. 21, 1979	EAGLE	Feb. 22, 1981	EAGLE
Oct. 4, 1979	RABBIT	Mar. 7, 1981	RABBIT
Oct. 17, 1979	TURTLE	Mar. 20, 1981	TURTLE
Oct. 30, 1979	PANTHER	Apr. 2, 1981	PANTHER
Nov. 12, 1979	DEER	Apr. 15, 1981	DEER
Nov. 25, 1979	FLOWER	Apr. 28, 1981	FLOWER

May 11, 1981	I	REED	Oct. 13, 1982	I	REED
May 24, 1981	I	TWINS	Oct. 26, 1982	I	TWINS
Jun. 6, 1981	I	REDBIRD	Nov. 8, 1982	I	REDBIRD
Jun. 19, 1981	I	RATTLESNAKE TOOTH	Nov. 21, 1982	I	RATTLESNAKE TOOTH
Jul. 2, 1981	I	SERPENT	Dec. 4, 1982	I	SERPENT
Jul. 15, 1981	I	FLINT	Dec. 17, 1982	I	FLINT
Jul. 28, 1981	I	RACCOON	Dec. 30, 1982	I	RACCOON
Aug. 10, 1981	I	DRAGON	Jan. 12, 1983	I	DRAGON
Aug. 23, 1981	I	HERON	Jan. 25, 1983	I	HERON
Sept. 5, 1981	I	WOLF	Feb. 7, 1983	I	WOLF
Sept. 18, 1981	I	HEARTH	Feb. 20, 1983	I	HEARTH
Oct. 1, 1981	I	OWL	Mar. 5, 1983	I	OWL
Oct. 14, 1981	I	THE RIVER	Mar. 18, 1983	I	THE RIVER
Oct. 27, 1981	I	WHIRLWIND	Mar. 31, 1983	I	WHIRLWIND
Nov. 9, 1981	I	EAGLE	Apr. 13, 1983	I	EAGLE
Nov. 22, 1981	I	RABBIT	Apr. 26, 1983	I	RABBIT
Dec. 5, 1981	I	TURTLE	May 9, 1983	I	TURTLE
Dec. 18, 1981	I	PANTHER	May 22, 1983	I	PANTHER
Dec. 31, 1981	I	DEER	Jun. 4, 1983	I	DEER
Jan. 13, 1982	I	FLOWER	Jun. 17, 1983	I	FLOWER
Jan. 26, 1982	I	REED	Jun. 30, 1983	I	REED
Feb. 8, 1982	I	TWINS	Jul. 13, 1983	I	TWINS
Feb. 21, 1982	I	REDBIRD	Jul. 26, 1983	I	REDBIRD
Mar. 6, 1982	I	RATTLESNAKE TOOTH	Aug. 8, 1983	I	RATTLESNAKE TOOTH
Mar. 19, 1982	I	SERPENT	Aug. 21, 1983	I	SERPENT
Apr. 1, 1982	I	FLINT	Sept. 3, 1983	I	FLINT
Apr. 14, 1982	I	RACCOON	Sept. 16, 1983	I	RACCOON
Apr. 27, 1982	I	DRAGON	Sept. 29, 1983	I	DRAGON
May 10, 1982	I	HERON	Oct. 12, 1983	I	HERON
May 23, 1982	I	WOLF	Oct. 25, 1983	I	WOLF
Jun. 5, 1982	I	HEARTH	Nov. 7, 1983	I	HEARTH
Jun. 18, 1982	I	OWL	Nov. 20, 1983	I	OWL
Jul. 1, 1982	I	THE RIVER	Dec. 3, 1983	I	THE RIVER
Jul. 14, 1982	I	WHIRLWIND	Dec. 16, 1983	I	WHIRLWIND
Jul. 27, 1982	I	EAGLE	Dec. 29, 1983	I	EAGLE
Aug. 9, 1982	I	RABBIT	Jan. 11, 1984	I	RABBIT
Aug. 22, 1982	I	TURTLE	Jan. 24, 1984	I	TURTLE
Sept. 4, 1982	I	PANTHER	Feb. 6, 1984	I	PANTHER
Sept. 17, 1982	I	DEER	Feb. 19, 1984	I	DEER
Sept. 30, 1982	I	FLOWER	Mar. 3, 1984	I	FLOWER

Mar. 16, 1984	I	REED	Aug. 18, 1985	I	REED
Mar. 29, 1984	I	TWINS	Aug. 31, 1985	I	TWINS
Apr. 11, 1984	I	REDBIRD	Sept. 13, 1985	I	REDBIRD
Apr. 24, 1984	I	RATTLESNAKE TOOTH	Sept. 26, 1985	I	RATTLESNAKE TOOTH
May 7, 1984	I	SERPENT	Oct. 9, 1985	I	SERPENT
May 20, 1984	I	FLINT	Oct. 22, 1985	I	FLINT
Jun. 2, 1984	I	RACCOON	Nov. 4, 1985	I	RACCOON
Jun. 15, 1984	I	DRAGON	Nov. 17, 1985	I	DRAGON
Jun. 28, 1984	I	HERON	Nov. 30, 1985	I	HERON
Jul. 11, 1984	I	WOLF	Dec. 13, 1985	I	WOLF
Jul. 24, 1984	I	HEARTH	Dec. 26, 1985	I	HEARTH
Aug. 6, 1984	I	OWL	Jan. 8, 1986	I	OWL
Aug. 19, 1984	I	THE RIVER	Jan. 21, 1986	I	THE RIVER
Sept. 1, 1984	I	WHIRLWIND	Feb. 3, 1986	I	WHIRLWIND
Sept. 14, 1984	I	EAGLE	Feb. 16, 1986	I	EAGLE
Sept. 27, 1984	I	RABBIT	Mar. 1, 1986	I	RABBIT
Oct. 10, 1984	I	TURTLE	Mar. 14, 1986	I	TURTLE
Oct. 23, 1984	I	PANTHER	Mar. 27, 1986	I	PANTHER
Nov. 5, 1984	I	DEER	Apr. 9, 1986	I	DEER
Nov. 18, 1984	I	FLOWER	Apr. 22, 1986	I	FLOWER
Dec. 1, 1984	I	REED	May 5, 1986	I	REED
Dec. 14, 1984	I	TWINS	May 18, 1986	I	TWINS
Dec. 27, 1984	I	REDBIRD	May 31, 1986	I	REDBIRD
Jan. 9, 1985	I	RATTLESNAKE TOOTH	Jun. 13, 1986	I	RATTLESNAKE TOOTH
Jan. 22, 1985	I	SERPENT	Jun. 26, 1986	I	SERPENT
Feb. 4, 1985	I	FLINT	Jul. 9, 1986	I	FLINT
Feb. 17, 1985	I	RACCOON	Jul. 22, 1986	I	RACCOON
Mar. 2, 1985	I	DRAGON	Aug. 4, 1986	I	DRAGON
Mar. 15, 1985	I	HERON	Aug. 17, 1986	I	HERON
Mar. 28, 1985	I	WOLF	Aug. 30, 1986	I	WOLF
Apr. 10, 1985	I	HEARTH	Sept. 12, 1986	I	HEARTH
Apr. 23, 1985	I	OWL	Sept. 25, 1986	I	OWL
May 6, 1985	I	THE RIVER	Oct. 8, 1986	I	THE RIVER
May 19, 1985	I	WHIRLWIND	Oct. 21, 1986	I	WHIRLWIND
Jun. 1, 1985	I	EAGLE	Nov. 3, 1986	I	EAGLE
Jun. 14, 1985	I	RABBIT	Nov. 16, 1986	I	RABBIT
Jun. 27, 1985	I	TURTLE	Nov. 29, 1986	I	TURTLE
Jul. 10, 1985	I	PANTHER	Dec. 12, 1986	I	PANTHER
Jul. 23, 1985	I	DEER	Dec. 25, 1986	I	DEER
Aug. 5, 1985	I	FLOWER	Jan. 7, 1987	I	FLOWER

Jan. 20, 1987	I	REED	Jun. 23, 1988	I	REED
Feb. 2, 1987	I	TWINS	Jul. 6, 1988	I	TWINS
Feb. 15, 1987	I	REDBIRD	Jul. 19, 1988	I	REDBIRD
Feb. 28, 1987	I	RATTLESNAKE TOOTH	Aug. 1, 1988	I	RATTLESNAKE TOOTH
Mar. 13, 1987	I	SERPENT	Aug. 14, 1988	I	SERPENT
Mar. 26, 1987	I	FLINT	Aug. 27, 1988	I	FLINT
Apr. 8, 1987	I	RACCOON	Sept. 9, 1988	I	RACCOON
Apr. 21, 1987	I	DRAGON	Sept. 22, 1988	I	DRAGON
May 4, 1987	I	HERON	Oct. 5, 1988	I	HERON
May 17, 1987	I	WOLF	Oct. 18, 1988	I	WOLF
May 30, 1987	I	HEARTH	Oct. 31, 1988	I	HEARTH
Jun. 12, 1987	I	OWL	Nov. 13, 1988	I	OWL
Jun. 25, 1987	I	THE RIVER	Nov. 26, 1988	I	THE RIVER
Jul. 8, 1987	I	WHIRLWIND	Dec. 9, 1988	I	WHIRLWIND
Jul. 21, 1987	I	EAGLE	Dec. 22, 1988	I	EAGLE
Aug. 3, 1987	I	RABBIT	Jan. 4, 1989	I	RABBIT
Aug. 16, 1987	I	TURTLE	Jan. 17, 1989	I	TURTLE
Aug. 29, 1987	I	PANTHER	Jan. 30, 1989	I	PANTHER
Sept. 11, 1987	I	DEER	Feb. 12, 1989	I	DEER
Sept. 24, 1987	I	FLOWER	Feb. 25, 1989	I	FLOWER
Oct. 7, 1987	I	REED	Mar. 10, 1989	I	REED
Oct. 20, 1987	I	TWINS	Mar. 23, 1989	I	TWINS
Nov. 2, 1987	I	REDBIRD	Apr. 5, 1989	I	REDBIRD
Nov. 15, 1987	I	RATTLESNAKE TOOTH	Apr. 18, 1989	I	RATTLESNAKE TOOTH
Nov. 28, 1987	I	SERPENT	May 1, 1989	I	SERPENT
Dec. 11, 1987	I	FLINT	May 14, 1989	I	FLINT
Dec. 24, 1987	I	RACCOON	May 27, 1989	I	RACCOON
Jan. 6, 1988	I	DRAGON	Jun. 9, 1989	I	DRAGON
Jan. 19, 1988	I	HERON	Jun. 22, 1989	I	HERON
Feb. 1, 1988	I	WOLF	Jul. 5, 1989	I	WOLF
Feb. 14, 1988	I	HEARTH	Jul. 18, 1989	I	HEARTH
Feb. 27, 1988	I	OWL	Jul. 31, 1989	I	OWL
Mar. 11, 1988	I	THE RIVER	Aug. 13, 1989	I	THE RIVER
Mar. 24, 1988	I	WHIRLWIND	Aug. 26, 1989	I	WHIRLWIND
Apr. 6, 1988	I	EAGLE	Sept. 8, 1989	I	EAGLE
Apr. 19, 1988	I	RABBIT	Sept. 21, 1989	I	RABBIT
May 2, 1988	I	TURTLE	Oct. 4, 1989	I	TURTLE
May 15, 1988	I	PANTHER	Oct. 17, 1989	I	PANTHER
May 28, 1988	I	DEER	Oct. 30, 1989	I	DEER
Jun. 10, 1988	I	FLOWER	Nov. 12, 1989	I	FLOWER

Nov. 25, 1989	REED	Apr. 29, 1991	REED
Dec. 8, 1989	TWINS	May 12, 1991	TWINS
Dec. 21, 1989	REDBIRD	May 25, 1991	REDBIRD
Jan. 3, 1990	RATTLESNAKE TOOTH	Jun. 7, 1991	RATTLESNAKE TOOTH
Jan. 16, 1990	SERPENT	Jun. 20, 1991	SERPENT
Jan. 29, 1990	FLINT	Jul. 3, 1991	FLINT
Feb. 11, 1990	RACCOON	Jul. 16, 1991	RACCOON
Feb. 24, 1990	DRAGON	Jul. 29, 1991	DRAGON
Mar. 9, 1990	HERON	Aug. 11, 1991	HERON
Mar. 22, 1990	WOLF	Aug. 24, 1991	WOLF
Apr. 4, 1990	HEARTH	Sept. 6, 1991	HEARTH
Apr. 17, 1990	OWL	Sept. 19, 1991	OWL
Apr. 30, 1990	THE RIVER	Oct. 2, 1991	THE RIVER
May 13, 1990	WHIRLWIND	Oct. 15, 1991	WHIRLWIND
May 26, 1990	EAGLE	Oct. 28, 1991	EAGLE
Jun. 8, 1990	RABBIT	Nov. 10, 1991	RABBIT
Jun. 21, 1990	TURTLE	Nov. 23, 1991	TURTLE
Jul. 4, 1990	PANTHER	Dec. 6, 1991	PANTHER
Jul. 17, 1990	DEER	Dec. 19, 1991	DEER
Jul. 30, 1990	FLOWER	Jan. 1, 1992	FLOWER
Aug. 12, 1990	REED	Jan. 14, 1992	REED
Aug. 25, 1990	TWINS	Jan. 27, 1992	TWINS
Sept. 7, 1990	REDBIRD	Feb. 9, 1992	REDBIRD
Sept. 20, 1990	RATTLESNAKE TOOTH	Feb. 22, 1992	RATTLESNAKE TOOTH
Oct. 3, 1990	SERPENT	Mar. 6, 1992	SERPENT
Oct. 16, 1990	FLINT	Mar. 19, 1992	FLINT
Oct. 29, 1990	RACCOON	Apr. 1, 1992	RACCOON
Nov. 11, 1990	DRAGON	Apr. 14, 1992	DRAGON
Nov. 24, 1990	HERON	Apr. 27, 1992	HERON
Dec. 7, 1990	WOLF	May 10, 1992	WOLF
Dec. 20, 1990	HEARTH	May 23, 1992	HEARTH
Jan. 2, 1991	OWL	Jun. 5, 1992	OWL
Jan. 15, 1991	THE RIVER	Jun. 18, 1992	THE RIVER
Jan. 28, 1991	WHIRLWIND	Jul. 1, 1992	WHIRLWIND
Feb. 10, 1991	EAGLE	Jul. 14, 1992	EAGLE
Feb. 23, 1991	RABBIT	Jul. 27, 1992	RABBIT
Mar. 8, 1991	TURTLE	Aug. 9, 1992	TURTLE
Mar. 21, 1991	PANTHER	Aug. 22, 1992	PANTHER
Apr. 3, 1991	DEER	Sept. 4, 1992	DEER
Apr. 16, 1991	FLOWER	Sept. 17, 1992	FLOWER

Sept. 30, 1992	I	REED	Mar. 4, 1994	I	REED
Oct. 13, 1992	I	TWINS	Mar. 17, 1994	I	TWINS
Oct. 26, 1992	I	REDBIRD	Mar. 30, 1994	I	REDBIRD
Nov. 8, 1992	I	RATTLESNAKE TOOTH	Apr. 12, 1994	I	RATTLESNAKE TOOTH
Nov. 21, 1992	I	SERPENT	Apr. 25, 1994	I	SERPENT
Dec. 4, 1992	I	FLINT	May 8, 1994	I	FLINT
Dec. 17, 1992	I	RACCOON	May 21, 1994	I	RACCOON
Dec. 30, 1992	I	DRAGON	Jun. 3, 1994	I	DRAGON
Jan. 12, 1993	I	HERON	Jun. 16, 1994	I	HERON
Jan. 25, 1993	I	WOLF	Jun. 29, 1994	I	WOLF
Feb. 7, 1993	I	HEARTH	Jul. 12, 1994	I	HEARTH
Feb. 20, 1993	I	OWL	Jul. 25, 1994	I	OWL
Mar. 5, 1993	I	THE RIVER	Aug. 7, 1994	I	THE RIVER
Mar. 18, 1993	I	WHIRLWIND	Aug. 20, 1994	I	WHIRLWIND
Mar. 31, 1993	I	EAGLE	Sept. 2, 1994	I	EAGLE
Apr. 13, 1993	I	RABBIT	Sept. 15, 1994	I	RABBIT
Apr. 26, 1993	I	TURTLE	Sept. 28, 1994	I	TURTLE
May 9, 1993	I	PANTHER	Oct. 11, 1994	I	PANTHER
May 22, 1993	I	DEER	Oct. 24, 1994	I	DEER
Jun. 4, 1993	I	FLOWER	Nov. 6, 1994	I	FLOWER
Jun. 17, 1993	I	REED	Nov. 19, 1994	I	REED
Jun. 30, 1993	I	TWINS	Dec. 2, 1994	I	TWINS
Jul. 13, 1993	I	REDBIRD	Dec. 15, 1994	I	REDBIRD
Jul. 26, 1993	I	RATTLESNAKE TOOTH	Dec. 28, 1994	I	RATTLESNAKE TOOTH
Aug. 8, 1993	I	SERPENT	Jan. 10, 1995	I	SERPENT
Aug. 21, 1993	I	FLINT	Jan. 23, 1995	I	FLINT
Sept. 3, 1993	I	RACCOON	Feb. 5, 1995	I	RACCOON
Sept. 16, 1993	I	DRAGON	Feb. 18, 1995	I	DRAGON
Sept. 29, 1993	I	HERON	Mar. 3, 1995	I	HERON
Oct. 12, 1993	I	WOLF	Mar. 16, 1995	I	WOLF
Oct. 25, 1993	I	HEARTH	Mar. 29, 1995	I	HEARTH
Nov. 7, 1993	I	OWL	Apr. 11, 1995	I	OWL
Nov. 20, 1993	I	THE RIVER	Apr. 24, 1995	I	THE RIVER
Dec. 3, 1993	I	WHIRLWIND	May 7, 1995	I	WHIRLWIND
Dec. 16, 1993	I	EAGLE	May 20, 1995	I	EAGLE
Dec. 29, 1993	I	RABBIT	Jun. 2, 1995	I	RABBIT
Jan. 11, 1994	I	TURTLE	Jun. 15, 1995	I	TURTLE
Jan. 24, 1994	I	PANTHER	Jun. 28, 1995	I	PANTHER
Feb. 6, 1994	I	DEER	Jul. 11, 1995	I	DEER
Feb. 19, 1994	I	FLOWER	Jul. 24, 1995	I	FLOWER

Aug. 6, 1995	REED	Jan. 7, 1997	REED
Aug. 19, 1995	TWINS	Jan. 20, 1997	TWINS
Sept. 1, 1995	REDBIRD	Feb. 2, 1997	REDBIRD
Sept. 14, 1995	RATTLESNAKE TOOTH	Feb. 15, 1997	RATTLESNAKE TOOTH
Sept. 27, 1995	SERPENT	Feb. 28, 1997	SERPENT
Oct. 10, 1995	FLINT	Mar. 13, 1997	FLINT
Oct. 23, 1995	RACCOON	Mar. 26, 1997	RACCOON
Nov. 5, 1995	DRAGON	Apr. 8, 1997	DRAGON
Nov. 18, 1995	HERON	Apr. 21, 1997	HERON
Dec. 1, 1995	WOLF	May 4, 1997	WOLF
Dec. 14, 1995	HEARTH	May 17, 1997	HEARTH
Dec. 27, 1995	OWL	May 30, 1997	OWL
Jan. 9, 1996	THE RIVER	Jun. 12, 1997	THE RIVER
Jan. 22, 1996	WHIRLWIND	Jun. 25, 1997	WHIRLWIND
Feb. 4, 1996	EAGLE	Jul. 8, 1997	EAGLE
Feb. 17, 1996	RABBIT	Jul. 21, 1997	RABBIT
Mar. 1, 1996	TURTLE	Aug. 3, 1997	TURTLE
Mar. 14, 1996	PANTHER	Aug. 16, 1997	PANTHER
Mar. 27, 1996	DEER	Aug. 29, 1997	DEER
Apr. 9, 1996	FLOWER	Sept. 11, 1997	FLOWER
Apr. 22, 1996	REED	Sept. 24, 1997	REED
May 5, 1996	TWINS	Oct. 7, 1997	TWINS
May 18, 1996	REDBIRD	Oct. 20, 1997	REDBIRD
May 31, 1996	RATTLESNAKE TOOTH	Nov. 2, 1997	RATTLESNAKE TOOTH
Jun. 13, 1996	SERPENT	Nov. 15, 1997	SERPENT
Jun. 26, 1996	FLINT	Nov. 28, 1997	FLINT
Jul. 9, 1996	RACCOON	Dec. 11, 1997	RACCOON
Jul. 22, 1996	DRAGON	Dec. 24, 1997	DRAGON
Aug. 4, 1996	HERON	Jan. 6, 1998	HERON
Aug. 17, 1996	WOLF	Jan. 19, 1998	WOLF
Aug. 30, 1996	HEARTH	Feb. 1, 1998	HEARTH
Sept. 12, 1996	OWL	Feb. 14, 1998	OWL
Sept. 25, 1996	THE RIVER	Feb. 27, 1998	THE RIVER
Oct. 8, 1996	WHIRLWIND	Mar. 12, 1998	WHIRLWIND
Oct. 21, 1996	EAGLE	Mar. 25, 1998	EAGLE
Nov. 3, 1996	RABBIT	Apr. 7, 1998	RABBIT
Nov. 16, 1996	TURTLE	Apr. 20, 1998	TURTLE
Nov. 29, 1996	PANTHER	May 3, 1998	PANTHER
Dec. 12, 1996	DEER	May 16, 1998	DEER
Dec. 25, 1996	FLOWER	May 29, 1998	FLOWER

Jun. 11, 1998	I	REED	Nov. 13, 1999	I	REED
Jun. 24, 1998	I	TWINS	Nov. 26, 1999	I	TWINS
Jul. 7, 1998	I	REDBIRD	Dec. 9, 1999	I	REDBIRD
Jul. 20, 1998	I	RATTLESNAKE TOOTH	Dec. 22, 1999	I	RATTLESNAKE TOOTH
Aug. 2, 1998	I	SERPENT	Jan. 4, 2000	I	SERPENT
Aug. 15, 1998	I	FLINT	Jan. 17, 2000	I	FLINT
Aug. 28, 1998	I	RACCOON	Jan. 30, 2000	I	RACCOON
Sept. 10, 1998	I	DRAGON	Feb. 12, 2000	I	DRAGON
Sept. 23, 1998	I	HERON	Feb. 25, 2000	I	HERON
Oct. 6, 1998	I	WOLF	Mar. 9, 2000	I	WOLF
Oct. 19, 1998	I	HEARTH	Mar. 22, 2000	I	HEARTH
Nov. 1, 1998	I	OWL	Apr. 4, 2000	I	OWL
Nov. 14, 1998	I	THE RIVER	Apr. 17, 2000	I	THE RIVER
Nov. 27, 1998	I	WHIRLWIND	Apr. 30, 2000	I	WHIRLWIND
Dec. 10, 1998	I	EAGLE	May 13, 2000	I	EAGLE
Dec. 23, 1998	I	RABBIT	May 26, 2000	I	RABBIT
Jan. 5, 1999	I	TURTLE	Jun. 8, 2000	I	TURTLE
Jan. 18, 1999	I	PANTHER	Jun. 21, 2000	I	PANTHER
Jan. 31, 1999	I	DEER	Jul. 4, 2000	I	DEER
Feb. 13, 1999	I	FLOWER	Jul. 17, 2000	I	FLOWER
Feb. 26, 1999	I	REED	Jul. 30, 2000	I	REED
Mar. 11, 1999	I	TWINS	Aug. 12, 2000	I	TWINS
Mar. 24, 1999	I	REDBIRD	Aug. 25, 2000	I	REDBIRD
Apr. 6, 1999	I	RATTLESNAKE TOOTH	Sept. 7, 2000	I	RATTLESNAKE TOOTH
Apr. 19, 1999	I	SERPENT	Sept. 20, 2000	I	SERPENT
May 2, 1999	I	FLINT	Oct. 3, 2000	I	FLINT
May 15, 1999	I	RACCOON	Oct. 16, 2000	I	RACCOON
May 28, 1999	I	DRAGON	Oct. 29, 2000	I	DRAGON
Jun. 10, 1999	I	HERON	Nov. 11, 2000	I	HERON
Jun. 23, 1999	I	WOLF	Nov. 24, 2000	I	WOLF
Jul. 6, 1999	I	HEARTH	Dec. 7, 2000	I	HEARTH
Jul. 19, 1999	I	OWL	Dec. 20, 2000	I	OWL
Aug. 1, 1999	I	THE RIVER	Jan. 2, 2001	I	THE RIVER
Aug. 14, 1999	I	WHIRLWIND	Jan. 15, 2001	I	WHIRLWIND
Aug. 27, 1999	I	EAGLE	Jan. 28, 2001	I	EAGLE
Sept. 9, 1999	I	RABBIT	Feb. 10, 2001	I	RABBIT
Sept. 22, 1999	I	TURTLE	Feb. 23, 2001	I	TURTLE
Oct. 5, 1999	I	PANTHER	Mar. 8, 2001	I	PANTHER
Oct. 18, 1999	I	DEER	Mar. 21, 2001	I	DEER
Oct. 31, 1999	I	FLOWER	Apr. 3, 2001	I	FLOWER

Apr. 16, 2001	I	REED
Apr. 29, 2001	I	TWINS
May 12, 2001	I	REDBIRD
May 25, 2001	I	RATTLESNAKE TOOTH
Jun. 7, 2001	I	SERPENT
Jun. 20, 2001	I	FLINT
Jul. 3, 2001	I	RACCOON
Jul. 16, 2001	I	DRAGON
Jul. 29, 2001	I	HERON
Aug. 11, 2001	I	WOLF
Aug. 24, 2001	I	HEARTH
Sept. 6, 2001	I	OWL
Sept. 19, 2001	I	THE RIVER
Oct. 2, 2001	I	WHIRLWIND
Oct. 15, 2001	I	EAGLE
Oct. 28, 2001	I	RABBIT
Nov. 10, 2001	I	TURTLE
Nov. 23, 2001	I	PANTHER
Dec. 6, 2001	I	DEER
Dec. 19, 2001	I	FLOWER
Jan. 1, 2002	I	REED
Jan. 14, 2002	I	TWINS
Jan. 27, 2002	I	REDBIRD
Feb. 9, 2002	I	RATTLESNAKE TOOTH
Feb. 22, 2002	I	SERPENT
Mar. 7, 2002	I	FLINT
Mar. 20, 2002	I	RACCOON
Apr. 2, 2002	I	DRAGON
Apr. 15, 2002	I	HERON
Apr. 28, 2002	I	WOLF
May 11, 2002	I	HEARTH
May 24, 2002	I	OWL
Jun. 6, 2002	I	THE RIVER
Jun. 19, 2002	I	WHIRLWIND
Jul. 2, 2002	I	EAGLE
Jul. 15, 2002	I	RABBIT
Jul. 28, 2002	I	TURTLE
Aug. 10, 2002	I	PANTHER
Aug. 23, 2002	I	DEER
Sept. 5, 2002	I	FLOWER

Sept. 18, 2002	I	REED
Oct. 1, 2002	I	TWINS
Oct. 14, 2002	I	REDBIRD
Oct. 27, 2002	I	RATTLESNAKE TOOTH
Nov. 9, 2002	I	SERPENT
Nov. 22, 2002	I	FLINT
Dec. 5, 2002	I	RACCOON
Dec. 18, 2002	I	DRAGON
Dec. 31, 2002	I	HERON
Jan. 13, 2003	I	WOLF
Jan. 26, 2003	I	HEARTH
Feb. 8, 2003	I	OWL
Feb. 21, 2003	I	THE RIVER
Mar. 6, 2003	I	WHIRLWIND
Mar. 19, 2003	I	EAGLE
Apr. 1, 2003	I	RABBIT
Apr. 14, 2003	I	TURTLE
Apr. 27, 2003	I	PANTHER
May 10, 2003	I	DEER
May 23, 2003	I	FLOWER
Jun. 5, 2003	I	REED
Jun. 18, 2003	I	TWINS
Jul. 1, 2003	I	REDBIRD
Jul. 14, 2003	I	RATTLESNAKE TOOTH
Jul. 27, 2003	I	SERPENT
Aug. 9, 2003	I	FLINT
Aug. 22, 2003	I	RACCOON
Sept. 4, 2003	I	DRAGON
Sept. 17, 2003	I	HERON
Sept. 30, 2003	I	WOLF
Oct. 13, 2003	I	HEARTH
Oct. 26, 2003	I	OWL
Nov. 8, 2003	I	THE RIVER
Nov. 21, 2003	I	WHIRLWIND
Dec. 4, 2003	I	EAGLE
Dec. 17, 2003	I	RABBIT
Dec. 30, 2003	I	TURTLE
Jan. 12, 2004	I	PANTHER
Jan. 25, 2004	I	DEER
Feb. 7, 2004	I	FLOWER

Feb. 20, 2004	I	REED	Jul. 24, 2005	I	REED
Mar. 4, 2004	I	TWINS	Aug. 6, 2005	I	TWINS
Mar. 17, 2004	I	REDBIRD	Aug. 19, 2005	I	REDBIRD
Mar. 30, 2004	I	RATTLESNAKE TOOTH	Sept. 1, 2005	I	RATTLESNAKE TOOTH
Apr. 12, 2004	I	SERPENT	Sept. 14, 2005	I	SERPENT
Apr. 25, 2004	I	FLINT	Sept. 27, 2005	I	FLINT
May 8, 2004	I	RACCOON	Oct. 10, 2005	I	RACCOON
May 21, 2004	I	DRAGON	Oct. 23, 2005	I	DRAGON
Jun. 3, 2004	I	HERON	Nov. 5, 2005	I	HERON
Jun. 16, 2004	I	WOLF	Nov. 18, 2005	I	WOLF
Jun. 29, 2004	I	HEARTH	Dec. 1, 2005	I	HEARTH
Jul. 12, 2004	I	OWL	Dec. 14, 2005	I	OWL
Jul. 25, 2004	I	THE RIVER	Dec. 27, 2005	I	THE RIVER
Aug. 7, 2004	I	WHIRLWIND	Jan. 9, 2006	I	WHIRLWIND
Aug. 20, 2004	I	EAGLE	Jan. 22, 2006	I	EAGLE
Sept. 2, 2004	I	RABBIT	Feb. 4, 2006	I	RABBIT
Sept. 15, 2004	I	TURTLE	Feb. 17, 2006	I	TURTLE
Sept. 28, 2004	I	PANTHER	Mar. 2, 2006	I	PANTHER
Oct. 11, 2004	I	DEER	Mar. 15, 2006	I	DEER
Oct. 24, 2004	I	FLOWER	Mar. 28, 2006	I	FLOWER
Nov. 6, 2004	I	REED	Apr. 10, 2006	I	REED
Nov. 19, 2004	I	TWINS	Apr. 23, 2006	I	TWINS
Dec. 2, 2004	I	REDBIRD	May 6, 2006	I	REDBIRD
Dec. 15, 2004	I	RATTLESNAKE TOOTH	May 19, 2006	I	RATTLESNAKE TOOTH
Dec. 28, 2004	I	SERPENT	Jun. 1, 2006	I	SERPENT
Jan. 10, 2005	I	FLINT	Jun. 14, 2006	I	FLINT
Jan. 23, 2005	I	RACCOON	Jun. 27, 2006	I	RACCOON
Feb. 5, 2005	I	DRAGON	Jul. 10, 2006	I	DRAGON
Feb. 18, 2005	I	HERON	Jul. 23, 2006	I	HERON
Mar. 3, 2005	I	WOLF	Aug. 5, 2006	I	WOLF
Mar. 16, 2005	I	HEARTH	Aug. 18, 2006	I	HEARTH
Mar. 29, 2005	I	OWL	Aug. 31, 2006	I	OWL
Apr. 11, 2005	I	THE RIVER	Sept. 13, 2006	I	THE RIVER
Apr. 24, 2005	I	WHIRLWIND	Sept. 26, 2006	I	WHIRLWIND
May 7, 2005	I	EAGLE	Oct. 9, 2006	I	EAGLE
May 20, 2005	I	RABBIT	Oct. 22, 2006	I	RABBIT
Jun. 2, 2005	I	TURTLE	Nov. 4, 2006	I	TURTLE
Jun. 15, 2005	I	PANTHER	Nov. 17, 2006	I	PANTHER
Jun. 28, 2005	I	DEER	Nov. 30, 2006	I	DEER
Jul. 11, 2005	I	FLOWER	Dec. 13, 2006	I	FLOWER

Dec. 26, 2006	REED	May 29, 2008	REED
Jan. 8, 2007	TWINS	Jun. 11, 2008	TWINS
Jan. 21, 2007	REDBIRD	Jun. 24, 2008	REDBIRD
Feb. 3, 2007	RATTLESNAKE TOOTH	Jul. 7, 2008	RATTLESNAKE TOOTH
Feb. 16, 2007	SERPENT	Jul. 20, 2008	SERPENT
Mar. 1, 2007	FLINT	Aug. 2, 2008	FLINT
Mar. 14, 2007	RACCOON	Aug. 15, 2008	RACCOON
Mar. 27, 2007	DRAGON	Aug. 28, 2008	DRAGON
Apr. 9, 2007	HERON	Sept. 10, 2008	HERON
Apr. 22, 2007	WOLF	Sept. 23, 2008	WOLF
May 5, 2007	HEARTH	Oct. 6, 2008	HEARTH
May 18, 2007	OWL	Oct. 19, 2008	OWL
May 31, 2007	THE RIVER	Nov. 1, 2008	THE RIVER
Jun. 13, 2007	WHIRLWIND	Nov. 14, 2008	WHIRLWIND
Jun. 26, 2007	EAGLE	Nov. 27, 2008	EAGLE
Jul. 9, 2007	RABBIT	Dec. 10, 2008	RABBIT
Jul. 22, 2007	TURTLE	Dec. 23, 2008	TURTLE
Aug. 4, 2007	PANTHER	Jan. 5, 2009	PANTHER
Aug. 17, 2007	DEER	Jan. 18, 2009	DEER
Aug. 30, 2007	FLOWER	Jan. 31, 2009	FLOWER
Sept. 12, 2007	REED	Feb. 13, 2009	REED
Sept. 25, 2007	TWINS	Feb. 26, 2009	TWINS
Oct. 8, 2007	REDBIRD	Mar. 11, 2009	REDBIRD
Oct. 21, 2007	RATTLESNAKE TOOTH	Mar. 24, 2009	RATTLESNAKE TOOTH
Nov. 3, 2007	SERPENT	Apr. 6, 2009	SERPENT
Nov. 16, 2007	FLINT	Apr. 19, 2009	FLINT
Nov. 29, 2007	RACCOON	May 2, 2009	RACCOON
Dec. 12, 2007	DRAGON	May 15, 2009	DRAGON
Dec. 25, 2007	HERON	May 28, 2009	HERON
Jan. 7, 2008	WOLF	Jun. 10, 2009	WOLF
Jan. 20, 2008	HEARTH	Jun. 23, 2009	HEARTH
Feb. 2, 2008	OWL	Jul. 6, 2009	OWL
Feb. 15, 2008	THE RIVER	Jul. 19, 2009	THE RIVER
Feb. 28, 2008	WHIRLWIND	Aug. 1, 2009	WHIRLWIND
Mar. 12, 2008	EAGLE	Aug. 14, 2009	EAGLE
Mar. 25, 2008	RABBIT	Aug. 27, 2009	RABBIT
Apr. 7, 2008	TURTLE	Sept. 9, 2009	TURTLE
Apr. 20, 2008	PANTHER	Sept. 22, 2009	PANTHER
May 3, 2008	DEER	Oct. 5, 2009	DEER
May 16, 2008	FLOWER	Oct. 18, 2009	FLOWER

Oct. 31, 2009	I	REED	Apr. 4, 2011	I	REED
Nov. 13, 2009	I	TWINS	Apr. 17, 2011	I	TWINS
Nov. 26, 2009	I	REDBIRD	Apr. 30, 2011	I	REDBIRD
Dec. 9, 2009	I	RATTLESNAKE TOOTH	May 13, 2011	I	RATTLESNAKE TOOTH
Dec. 22, 2009	I	SERPENT	May 26, 2011	I	SERPENT
Jan. 4, 2010	I	FLINT	Jun. 8, 2011	I	FLINT
Jan. 17, 2010	I	RACCOON	Jun. 21, 2011	I	RACCOON
Jan. 30, 2010	I	DRAGON	Jul. 4, 2011	I	DRAGON
Feb. 12, 2010	I	HERON	Jul. 17, 2011	I	HERON
Feb. 25, 2010	I	WOLF	Jul. 30, 2011	I	WOLF
Mar. 10, 2010	I	HEARTH	Aug. 12, 2011	I	HEARTH
Mar. 23, 2010	I	OWL	Aug. 25, 2011	I	OWL
Apr. 5, 2010	I	THE RIVER	Sept. 7, 2011	I	THE RIVER
Apr. 18, 2010	I	WHIRLWIND	Sept. 20, 2011	I	WHIRLWIND
May 1, 2010	I	EAGLE	Oct. 3, 2011	I	EAGLE
May 14, 2010	I	RABBIT	Oct. 16, 2011	I	RABBIT
May 27, 2010	I	TURTLE	Oct. 29, 2011	I	TURTLE
Jun. 9, 2010	I	PANTHER	Nov. 11, 2011	I	PANTHER
Jun. 22, 2010	I	DEER	Nov. 24, 2011	I	DEER
Jul. 5, 2010	I	FLOWER	Dec. 7, 2011	I	FLOWER
Jul. 18, 2010	I	REED	Dec. 20, 2011	I	REED
Jul. 31, 2010	I	TWINS	Jan. 2, 2012	I	TWINS
Aug. 13, 2010	I	REDBIRD	Jan. 15, 2012	I	REDBIRD
Aug. 26, 2010	I	RATTLESNAKE TOOTH	Jan. 28, 2012	I	RATTLESNAKE TOOTH
Sept. 8, 2010	I	SERPENT	Feb. 10, 2012	I	SERPENT
Sept. 21, 2010	I	FLINT	Feb. 23, 2012	I	FLINT
Oct. 4, 2010	I	RACCOON	Mar. 7, 2012	I	RACCOON
Oct. 17, 2010	I	DRAGON	Mar. 20, 2012	I	DRAGON
Oct. 30, 2010	I	HERON	Apr. 2, 2012	I	HERON
Nov. 12, 2010	I	WOLF	Apr. 15, 2012	I	WOLF
Nov. 25, 2010	I	HEARTH	Apr. 28, 2012	I	HEARTH
Dec. 8, 2010	I	OWL	May 11, 2012	I	OWL
Dec. 21, 2010	I	THE RIVER	May 24, 2012	I	THE RIVER
Jan. 3, 2011	I	WHIRLWIND	Jun. 6, 2012	I	WHIRLWIND
Jan. 16, 2011	I	EAGLE	Jun. 19, 2012	I	EAGLE
Jan. 29, 2011	I	RABBIT	Jul. 2, 2012	I	RABBIT
Feb. 11, 2011	I	TURTLE	Jul. 15, 2012	I	TURTLE
Feb. 24, 2011	I	PANTHER	Jul. 28, 2012	I	PANTHER
Mar. 9, 2011	I	DEER	Aug. 10, 2012	I	DEER
Mar. 22, 2011	I	FLOWER	Aug. 23, 2012	I	FLOWER

Sept. 5, 2012	REED	Feb. 7, 2014	REED
Sept. 18, 2012	TWINS	Feb. 20, 2014	TWINS
Oct. 1, 2012	REDBIRD	Mar. 5, 2014	REDBIRD
Oct. 14, 2012	RATTLESNAKE TOOTH	Mar. 18, 2014	RATTLESNAKE TOOTH
Oct. 27, 2012	SERPENT	Mar. 31, 2014	SERPENT
Nov. 9, 2012	FLINT	Apr. 13, 2014	FLINT
Nov. 22, 2012	RACCOON	Apr. 26, 2014	RACCOON
Dec. 5, 2012	DRAGON	May 9, 2014	DRAGON
Dec. 18, 2012	HERON	May 22, 2014	HERON
Dec. 31, 2012	WOLF	Jun. 4, 2014	WOLF
Jan. 13, 2013	HEARTH	Jun. 17, 2014	HEARTH
Jan. 26, 2013	OWL	Jun. 30, 2014	OWL
Feb. 8, 2013	THE RIVER	Jul. 13, 2014	THE RIVER
Feb. 21, 2013	WHIRLWIND	Jul. 26, 2014	WHIRLWIND
Mar. 6, 2013	EAGLE	Aug. 8, 2014	EAGLE
Mar. 19, 2013	RABBIT	Aug. 21, 2014	RABBIT
Apr. 1, 2013	TURTLE	Sept. 3, 2014	TURTLE
Apr. 14, 2013	PANTHER	Sept. 16, 2014	PANTHER
Apr. 27, 2013	DEER	Sept. 29, 2014	DEER
May 10, 2013	FLOWER	Oct. 12, 2014	FLOWER
May 23, 2013	REED	Oct. 25, 2014	REED
Jun. 5, 2013	TWINS	Nov. 7, 2014	TWINS
Jun. 18, 2013	REDBIRD	Nov. 20, 2014	REDBIRD
Jul. 1, 2013	RATTLESNAKE TOOTH	Dec. 3, 2014	RATTLESNAKE TOOTH
Jul. 14, 2013	SERPENT	Dec. 16, 2014	SERPENT
Jul. 27, 2013	FLINT	Dec. 29, 2014	FLINT
Aug. 9, 2013	RACCOON	Jan. 11, 2015	RACCOON
Aug. 22, 2013	DRAGON	Jan. 24, 2015	DRAGON
Sept. 4, 2013	HERON	Feb. 6, 2015	HERON
Sept. 17, 2013	WOLF	Feb. 19, 2015	WOLF
Sept. 30, 2013	HEARTH	Mar. 4, 2015	HEARTH
Oct. 13, 2013	OWL	Mar. 17, 2015	OWL
Oct. 26, 2013	THE RIVER	Mar. 30, 2015	THE RIVER
Nov. 8, 2013	WHIRLWIND	Apr. 12, 2015	WHIRLWIND
Nov. 21, 2013	EAGLE	Apr. 25, 2015	EAGLE
Dec. 4, 2013	RABBIT	May 8, 2015	RABBIT
Dec. 17, 2013	TURTLE	May 21, 2015	TURTLE
Dec. 30, 2013	PANTHER	Jun. 3, 2015	PANTHER
Jan. 12, 2014	DEER	Jun. 16, 2015	DEER
Jan. 25, 2014	FLOWER	Jun. 29, 2015	FLOWER

Jul. 12, 2015	REED	Oct. 11, 2015	DRAGON
Jul. 25, 2015	TWINS	Oct. 24, 2015	HERON
Aug. 7, 2015	REDBIRD	Nov. 6, 2015	WOLF
Aug. 20, 2015	RATTLESNAKE TOOTH	Nov. 19, 2015	HEARTH
		Dec. 2, 2015	OWL
Sept. 2, 2015	SERPENT	Dec. 15, 2015	THE RIVER
Sept. 15, 2015	FLINT	Dec. 28, 2015	WHIRLWIND
Sept. 28, 2015	RACCOON		

BOOKS OF RELATED INTEREST

Walking on the Wind
Cherokee Teachings for Harmony and Balance
by Michael Tlanusta Garrett

Medicine of the Cherokee
The Way of Right Relationship
by J. T. Garrett and Michael Tlanusta Garrett

The Cherokee Full Circle
A Practical Guide to Ceremonies and Traditions
by J. T. Garrett and Michael Tlanusta Garrett

The Cherokee Herbal
Native Plant Medicine from the Four Directions
by J. T. Garrett

Meditations with the Cherokee
Prayers, Songs, and Stories of Healing and Harmony
by J. T. Garrett

Bird Medicine
The Sacred Power of Bird Shamanism
by Evan T. Pritchard

Aspects in Astrology
A Guide to Understanding Planetary Relationships in the Horoscope
by Sue Tompkins

Moon Phase Astrology
The Lunar Key to Your Destiny
by Raven Kaldera

Inner Traditions • Bear & Company
P.O. Box 388
Rochester, VT 05767
1-800-246-8648
www.InnerTraditions.com

Or contact your local bookseller